BEING HINDU IN BANGLADESH

Also by Deep Halder

Blood Island: An Oral History of the Marichjhapi Massacre

Bengal 2021: An Election Diary

BEING HINDU IN BANGLADESH

An Untold Story

DEEP HALDER
AVISHEK BISWAS

HarperCollins *Publishers* India

First published in India by HarperCollins *Publishers* 2023
4th Floor, Tower A, Building No. 10, DLF Cyber City,
DLF Phase II, Gurugram, Haryana – 122002
www.harpercollins.co.in

2 4 6 8 10 9 7 5 3 1

P-ISBN: 978-93-5699-580-2
E-ISBN: 978-93-5699-581-9

Typeset in 12/16 Adobe Garamond at
Manipal Technologies Limited, Manipal

Printed and bound at
Replika Press Pvt. Ltd.

MIX
Paper from responsible sources
FSC® C016779

This book is produced from independently certified FSC® paper to ensure responsible forest management.

To Smritikana Biswas,
who saw the 1946 Noakhali Riots and
survived to tell the tale

The detailed notes pertaining to this book are available on the HarperCollins *Publishers* India website. Scan this QR code to access the same.

CONTENTS

PREFACE

SMRITIKANA BISWAS WAS twelve when her father thought of killing her sister. The family was hiding inside a college building. Outside, the fire of religious hatred burned through Noakhali. The twelve-year-old had seen things nobody should see. Hacked bodies strewn on streets, houses on fire, raped women wailing. Other families were huddled together inside the college building as well, praying that the mad pack of murderous men would somehow not find them. But who would explain the extent of danger to Smritikana's seven-month-old sister? The little one just wouldn't keep quiet, her wails could bring the rioters in. Hand-on-mouth, tight hug, treacle—nothing would stop her. 'Maybe, we have to kill her to save ourselves,' Smritikana's father said. Horror-struck at what he said he would do, and what would happen if he didn't, Smritikana shuddered.

It was October 1946, and the place—Noakhali—was then in undivided India and now in Bangladesh. Smritikana Biswas, now almost ninety, is the grandmother of Avishek Biswas, the co-author of this book.

We are the sons and grandsons of refugees. Avishek and I (Deep Halder) were born thirteen years apart in the eastern Indian state of West Bengal. Our parents, and their parents before them, were born on what lay to the east of West Bengal, which is now the independent country Bangladesh. When they were born, there was no West Bengal and Bangladesh. There was one big Bengal. When they left, hearts and homes had been partitioned, hope hacked, a province ripped into two.

The eastern part of Bengal became East Bengal first with the Partition of India in 1947. And then, it was renamed East Pakistan after 1955. This land snatched its bloody freedom from West Pakistan in 1971 and became Bangladesh. In all this, the back stories of Avishek's parents and mine were blown away like grains of sand in the wind. And Bangladesh remained another country.

Growing up, my 'Bangal' identity,[1] would come up every once in a while—in the slightly different tongue my grandmother would speak (she was from Barishal district in south-central Bangladesh) and the odd jibes my friends in school would casually throw at me and the other Bangals in class. 'If all Bangals are from zamindar families in East Bengal before the Partition, pray who were the subjects?' they would say. I would hear the chatter about Banglas and Ghotis,[2]—spicing their cuisines differently, not marrying each other and so on. The differences, if not always the hostility, even spilled over to the football field with the Bangals and the Ghotis having their own football clubs named East Bengal and Mohan Bagan respectively; the 1976 film *Mohonbaganer Meye* touched upon the subject.

But, for me, that is where the refugee experience ended. Growing up with relative privilege in the home of a professor father and a banker mother, the Partition was at best an occasional bedtime story and Bangladesh a country that was once known by another name, where my parents came from. My parents shielded me from the horror they kept hidden in their hearts.

For Avishek, though, the refugee experience was too real to gloss over. The stink of an open drain, the sweat of a community cramped together in Netaji Nagar Colony—it was a congested, unauthorized refugee settlement just outside Kolkata. He witnessed the struggle of a father who had to carry a big bag of incense-stick packets that his (Avishek's) mother and grandmother, Smritikana, would make at home to sell to shops in Kolkata. Having lost everything to the Partition, Avishek's family toiled to make ends meet and make something of their only son. Perhaps because of this lived reality and the stories he heard as a child of why they were the way they were, Avishek chose oral narratives of the Dalit Partition survivors as the topic for his PhD thesis. And perhaps it was the refugee blood in him that compelled him to reach out to me after I wrote my first book, *Blood Island: An Oral History of the*

Marichjhapi Massacre.[3] It was on the plight of a band of Dalit Hindu refugees, who escaped persecution and almost certain death in East Pakistan and fled to West Bengal, only to be massacred by the police under the Left government in 1978–79.

Avishek and I became fast friends, trading stories and planning trips to Bangladesh to see what is left of our origin stories and thinking, maybe, to put pen to paper and write what we see. But I felt a sense of disquiet when a copy of the Quran was found at the feet of Lord Hanuman's statue at Nanua Dighir Par puja pandal in Bangladesh's Comilla district on 13 October 2021, and Muslim mobs took to the streets attacking Hindu temples, breaking idols, breaking into Hindu homes and setting their property on fire.[4] My day job as online editor of *India Today* requires me to report the news first and feel later even if the news is about grave calamities. But this was different. What started in Comilla with murderous mobs attacking Hindus, had spread to other parts of Bangladesh, even Noakhali.

Smritikana's nightmares were becoming news again.

Avishek and I decided it was time not just to travel to Bangladesh together, but also to begin writing about a land that was home to our families once and is now a memory. To write about people whose last names still make them vulnerable to extremism today, in much the same way that it made our parents and grandparents vulnerable and afraid many decades ago and forced them to flee. We thought of a long narrative piece for a newspaper, but did not know it would become a book.

Many trips and a year later, when we met Mukta Saha (her name changed to Mukta Das after marriage) in Noakhali, she asked us where we were when they were being attacked. 'We?' we asked incredulously. 'When neighbours become murderers, shouldn't strangers come to save us?' she asked us. She had lost much to the 2021 anti-Hindu violence and simply said, 'We died last year. What you see are corpses.'[5]

As we began our journey not just through the length and breadth of Bangladesh but also through the bloody pages of its history, we met many Muktas. In Dhaka, we met Purnima Rani Shil, who bore the brunt of being a Hindu and working for Bangladesh's current Prime Minister Sheikh Hasina's party, the Awami League. In 2001, the coalition led by the Bangladesh Nationalist Party (BNP) and the Bangladesh Jamaat-e-Islami (popularly known as Jamaat) won the general election, replacing the Awami League. This led to the 2001 Bangladesh post-election violence, during which the Awami League supporters and members of religious minorities were targeted by the BNP and Jamaat activists.

Purnima Shil, then twelve-years-old, was targeted as she was a polling agent of the Awami League and had also protested ballot-stuffing by the BNP activists during the election. She lived in Perba Delua in Ullahpara upazila, Sirajganj district. Her home was attacked by thirty to forty men on 8 October 2001. She was gang raped. Four people, associated with the BNP and Jamaat, were arrested but never charged. Her sister lost her eyesight and the family business (a saloon) was looted twice. Her family was forced to flee the village. This was part of a systematic attack by radical Islamists and the Jamaat on Hindu villages to drive their residents out of Bangladesh.

The countryside was no longer safe for her and she went to Dhaka, where she met Sheikh Hasina, then opposition leader. Hasina asked Purnima to stay with her. 'I call her "Mamoni". She did for me what my relatives didn't. She cared for me as if I was her own,' Purnima tells us. Why, then, is she not happy with Hasina today? (See chapter 2, 'Horror in the Countryside'.)

In Dhaka, I met the President of Bangladesh, Mohammad Shahabuddin Chuppu. In December 2006 following a High Court order, a three-member judicial commission was formed to look into the 2001 anti-Hindu violence led by the BNP and Jamaat. It was led by former District and Sessions Judge Mohammad Shahabuddin Chuppu![6]

'Yes, I travelled across Bangladesh to record the statements of victims,' the President said. 'I remember Purnima Rani Shil. Her case drew international attention. But there were hundreds of others. I met Hindu women raped so many times during that wave of anti-Hindu violence that they lost their minds. I feel what happened in 2001 was even worse than what happened in 1971 during the Bangladesh Liberation War.'

But was it just the BNP and Jamaat that were to blame? The 2021 anti-Hindu violence and the attacks happened under Sheikh Hasina's watch. Her party and her government swear by secularism. So what gives? In chapter 3, 'The DNA of Hate', we take a hard look at Bangladesh's social fissures and the heat of Islamist hate that is rising through the cracks to engulf the society at large. When I interviewed Bangladesh Home Minister Asaduzzaman Khan, he laid the blame on the Jamaat camp: 'They targeted and killed the intellectuals of Bangladesh. At present they are banned from participating in the politics of Bangladesh and trust me their number is getting smaller by the day.'

But the rot, as we found out, runs deeper. Thirty years from now, no Hindus will be left in Bangladesh should the current rate of exodus continue. 'The rate of exodus over the past forty-nine years points in that direction,' predicts Dr Abul Barkat, a Dhaka University professor. On an average, as of 2016, 632 people from the minority community leave the country each day.[7]

If section I of this book is about the fissures in Bangladesh's socio-religious fabric, section II is about fusion. Like most countries in South Asia, if one hypothesis is found to be true, the exact opposite is almost always true as well. A strong argument can be made that Hindus are under siege in Bangladesh. But an equally strong counterargument can be put out that Hinduism is alive and thriving in the country.

How many people know today that the first law and labour minister of independent Pakistan was a Dalit Hindu named Jogendranath Mandal? We travelled to Mandal's old house, now a ruin, in the village of his birth, now in

Bangladesh's Barishal district. Curiously, Muslims and Hindus of that dusty hamlet still hold on to his dream of religious unity, of a country where Muslims may be in majority, but Hindus can also live in peace with many gods. (See chapter 4, 'The Burnt Forehead of Jogen Mandal'.)

It is not just about Hindus occupying top positions in government, bureaucracy, police and industry in Bangladesh even today, but the many ancient strands of the religion that continue to coexist with the religious belief of Bangladesh's majority population. The most famous YouTuber from Bangladesh, Salahuddin Sumon, shoots videos about the Hindu temples in Bangladesh, digs into their history and mythology. Why does he do that? 'Whenever I go back in time and try to dig up our past, I come across the Hindu temples. I have been asked often why I am obsessed with Hindu temples. The answer is my love for history. The story of Bangladesh's temples fascinates me,' he said. (See chapter 5, 'Roots, Shoots and Sermons'.)

But what happens when this love for each other translates into marriage? Looking out from the terrace of her apartment in Dhaka's posh Dhanmondi area, actress Ashna Habib Bhabna said, 'Animesh is seventeen years older than me. And he is Hindu. But in our journey together, as friendship gradually turned to love, these things didn't matter.' But society? 'Society tries to cage you, yes. I hear taunts from colleagues, concerned questions from friends, but am I not the perfect example of Hindu-Muslim love?' Is she? Or is that simply privilege talking? Can interfaith love survive outside the charmed circles of Dhaka's social elites? (See chapter 6, 'Loving the Other in Bangladesh'.)

In section III, we dig into the story of Bangladesh's origin. How and why East Pakistan fought to be something else—a new nation birthed from the massacre of millions. Many of them Bengali-Hindus who were ravaged, raped and reduced to mere numbers in a genocide that the rest of the world turned their face away from. The blood of Bengali-Muslims was also spilled, those who stood against the tyranny of West Pakistan, and rejected Urdu for their mother tongue Bangla.

And from their supreme sacrifice, Bangladesh was born.

It was conceived as a country for both the Hindus and Muslims, and others with Bangla as the common language, with Bengali culture acting as the glue between citizens of different faiths. What was it like then? And did the war for a secular state that began in 1971 end with the birth of Bangladesh? (See chapter 7, '1971 Has Not Ended'.)

Sheikh Mujibur Rahman famously said:

> This country does not belong to Hindus. This country does not belong to Muslims. Whoever thinks this country is theirs, this country will be theirs. Whoever will feel happiness seeing this country prosper, this country will be theirs. Whoever will cry seeing this country sad, this country will be theirs. This country will also belong to those who have given away everything for this country's freedom and would do so in the future.

On 27 January 1952, when Khwaja Nazimuddin, then Prime Minister of Pakistan, declared Urdu to be the only national language of Pakistan, protests from all corners flared up in East Bengal, reaching a peak on 21 February, when lakhs of students gathered at the campuses of Dhaka University and other educational institutions in the city. It was a civil disobedience movement for language. The police became so violent that it started firing on protesting students and many were grievously injured. The government had to deploy the army to control the situation on the ground.

A secular Bengali identity was overshadowing the religious identities of the people. East Bengal was morphing, becoming more than what West Pakistan wanted it to be—soul searching, shape-shifting into something else. Then, the Awami Muslim League became the Awami League by dropping the word 'Muslim'. The year was 1953. Mujibur Rahman was one of the most influential minds behind this change. Years and many tears later, the country became Bangladesh and Mujib's dream was realized.

But in this subcontinent's history, peace turns to pieces like a dropped porcelain plate on a hard floor. On 15 August 1975, Mujibur Rahman and many of his family members were assassinated by those who did not believe in his idea of Bangladesh. Bangabandhu (an honorific prefix given to Rahman, meaning 'friend of Bengal') had been taking steps to start the process of toning down religious fundamentalism in Bangladesh. This made his enemies so furious that they wanted to overthrow and kill Rahman 'with 28 tanks, eighteen 105 mm guns and 700 men'. And they did.

Today, Mujibur Rahman's daughter, Shiekh Hasina, is in power. She is Bangladesh's longest-serving Prime Minister and the country has seen impressive growth under her, especially during the Global Financial Crisis when it achieved a 5.5 per cent annual growth rate between 2007 and 2009 against a global average of 0.4 per cent.

In our travels across Bangladesh, we marvelled at the roads, the highways and, at Hasina's dream project, the Swapner Padma Setu—a two-level road-rail bridge across the Padma River. But has she been able to realize her father's dream of a secular Bangladesh? The going has not been easy for her. It has been a long journey to reclaim Bangladesh's soul from dictators and fundamentalists; to put balm on the battered soul of the country's minority Hindu population that has gone down from 13.5 per cent in 1974 to 8.5 per cent in 2022.[8]

In the process she has survived many assassination attempts, been the subject of unflattering headlines from the press, both local and international, and has come under sharp attack from her political detractors—often in unmentionable language on the streets and social media. But if Hindus feel unsafe in her country even today, if attacks on their homes and temples continue, can she deflect the blame? (Chapter 8, 'A Father's Dream, a Daughter's Challenge'.)

How many interviews does it take to tell the story of people? How many books should one read to get a grasp of the country where faiths collide? How many trips are enough to write a book about a land that is not one's own?

I do not know. What I do know is that in my journey to tell the story of the land of my forefathers, I could not have found a better co-passenger than Avishek Biswas, nor a better guide than Sahidul Hasan Khokon, India Today Group's Bangladesh correspondent. He took us through not just Bangladesh's power corridors, but made us see that side of Bangladesh where the Muslims and Hindus celebrate each other's festivals and despise the rising hate of religious intolerance in the country.

So what did we learn as our journey ended? That beyond the certitude of power and the righteousness of religion, is the love of language. '*Ora toh Bangla-y kotha bole* (They speak in Bangla),' Smritikana Biswas had told me and Avishek when we informed her of our travel plans, her mind drifting away from her Netaji Nagar room.

It was Bangla that had turned East Pakistan into Bangladesh.

Maybe Bangla will save Bangladesh.

—Deep Halder
Dhaka
April 2023

I

FISSURE

1

NOAKHALI: 1946, 2021

MOHANDAS KARAMCHAND GANDHI'S goat went missing from this village. The apostle of peace had come to appeal for peace. Instead, they took away the goat he loved to feed with his own hands and the whole village had a feast. We don't know who those people were, nor can we find out if this story is true. This was in 1946 and far more serious matters were at hand than finding out the truth about a lost goat.

It was a funny story to hear as we stand inside Gandhi Ashram in Sonaimuri, a sub-district of Noakhali district in Bangladesh, seventy-six years after Gandhi tried to stop villagers from killing fellow villagers here and one year after the communal fire singed Noakhali and other parts of Bangladesh during Durga Puja.

It is drizzling outside and we have come to this sleepy village after a five-hour-drive from Dhaka. A white statue of Gandhi stands outside a building, looking over green fields, shallow ponds, quacking ducks and curious villagers. Inside the red-brick building that has been turned into a memorial museum for Gandhi and his time in Noakhali—with photographs, used utensils, a replica of his bed, and the famous spinning wheel—we ask Raha Naba Kumar, Director of Gandhi Ashram Trust that runs this place, the truth about the goat. It was one of the men who works with Raha in the ashram, who had told us the story. Raha smiles, and perhaps in keeping with his exalted status at the ashram, neither confirms nor denies the story and invites us for lunch.

Over steaming khichdi, fried brinjals and egg curry, he tells us how Noakhali had shaken Gandhi. According to the record, Gandhi had travelled to the riot-hit villages and pleaded with Muslims to be part of peace committees instead of rioting gangs. To the Muslim villagers of Fatehpur, he said that it was the easiest thing to harass the Hindus as Muslims were in the majority. He had asked them to show him if the Quran had ever suggested such a thing. No one listened to him and Noakhali descended into darkness. On 17 February 1947, a local religious leader, Maulvi Khalilur Rahman told Gandhi that religious conversion was the only way to save the Hindus. And those who didn't change, their gods would fall to the sword.[1] And they did.

And yet again, more than seven decades later, in 2021, it was the goddess that fell to the sword in Noakhali. Broken Goddess Durga idols lay on streets outside pandals as mobs went on rampage against Hindus. The youth in this district may not know much about what happened in 1946 that made Gandhi come here, but for the older population October 2021 brought back old horrors.

A copy of the Quran was found at the feet of Lord Hanuman's statue at Nanua Dighir Par puja pandal in neighbouring Comilla district on 13 October 2021. No Hindu had done it, superintendent of police, Comilla, Farooq Ahmed, told news media later. The man who did this was a local resident—thirty-five-year-old Iqbal Hossain.[2] But it lit fires across Bangladesh through social media platforms. Muslim mobs took to streets attacking Hindu temples, breaking idols, breaking into Hindu homes and setting their property on fire. Lives were lost, houses and temples burnt, indignity rubbed in the face of the Hindu minority population.

The news travelled beyond borders. Indian news site 'The Quint' said the following its report published on 19 October 2021: 'Although the fire of religious hatred and persecution was lit by pre-Partition players, especially the Muslim League in their demand for a separate country, the ongoing incidents prove that religious hatred still burns red in Bangladesh, making the life of Bengali Hindu minorities miserable.'[3]

The Daily Star, the largest-circulating daily English-language newspaper in Bangladesh, reported that 117 Hindu temples or puja pandals and 301 shops/homes were also damaged after the Comilla incident.[4] One particularly disturbing video that was shared widely on social media showed a ransacked pandal in Noakhali—broken chairs, a half-burnt pyre. A priest was seen performing puja seated on the road in front of the pandal with whatever was left of the idol of Goddess Durga. Devotees were sitting around him, hands folded, tears dried. Bangladesh Foreign Minister A.K. Abdul Momen told the press that six people were killed in the violence, two from Noakhali itself, but news of rapes was false.[5]

As we finish our lunch, Raha says, 'I am old enough to remember what happened in Noakhali in 1946. How it remained a deep scar in Gandhi's heart long after things went back to normal. Those memories came flooding back.'

Our lunch with Raha at the Gandhi Ashram is over. A bunch of schoolgirls in burqa enter one of the rooms in the museum building and peer closely at a picture of Gandhi with Jinnah. From a little distance we see them looking at the picture where Gandhi is watching Jinnah. What did Gandhi see when he saw Jinnah?

What did he hear when Muhammad Ali Jinnah, then leader of the All India Muslim League, announced that 16 August 1946 would be 'Direct Action Day' and warned the Congress: 'We do not want war. If you want war we accept your offer unhesitatingly. We will either have a divided India or a destroyed India.'[6]

Could Gandhi foresee that since the moment Jinnah wanted Pakistan, Calcutta (now Kolkata) would have to pay the price?

In August 1946, as bodies lined the streets of Calcutta and shrieks of raped women shattered the silence of the night, an unlikely figure emerged as a saviour of the Hindus. The owner of a local meat shop—a butcher who worshipped Goddess Kali—picked up his cleaver and took the fight to the marauding gangs who interpreted Jinnah's call for direct action as annihilation of Hindus. The butcher, Gopal Patha, would become a footnote of history, will be referred to as communal bigot by later-day historians. In 1947, as communal tensions still ran high, Gandhi would come down to Calcutta and appeal to Patha to lay down arms. Patha had no patience for Gandhi's 'if someone slaps you on one side of your face, turn the other one to him' sermon. He had a retort ready: 'I will not lay down, even a nail, if it has been used to defend Hindu honour.'[7]

Raha's team member, the man who told us the story of Gandhi's stolen goat in Noakhali, says: 'For us, in Noakhali, last year's Durga Puja violence felt like Jinnah coming back to life. And there was no Gopal Patha around.'

The Great Calcutta Killings had halted Jinnah's plans, but the fire of communalism erupted again in Noakhali on 10 October 1946. It was the day of Kojagori Lakkhi Puja. In Bengali, Kojagori means '*ke jaago re*' or 'who is awake'? Lakkhi (more popularly known as 'Lakshmi') is the goddess of wealth and well-being. On that day, her worshippers in Noakhali lost their wealth, well-being and much more.

Up until that year, Noakhali—despite being the youngest district in the Gangetic delta—was prosperous. A district with canals and trees, rather typical of the eastern

Bengal countryside, Noakhali was one of the most postcard-perfect and agriculturally fertile districts. But by the year end, Noakhali became a wasteland.

What happened in Calcutta in August 1946 had a direct effect on the Hindus in Noakhali two months later. By then, Gandhi had a sense of the shape of things to come and had said, 'We are not yet in the midst of a civil war, but we are nearing it. At present we are playing at it.'[8]

'Remembering the horrific incidents, Raha says, Thankfully, 2021 Durga Puja violence, however horrific, was not a civil war like 1946 nor genocide.' He adds, 'If Muslims came to kill and maim Hindus, other Muslims saved us.'

Aminul Hoq Munna was one of those 'other Muslims' who saved the day for Hindus in Noakhali. As joint convenor, Noakhali District Awami Jubo League, the youth wing of Prime Minister Sheikh Hasina's political party, Munna was ready for trouble as soon as news of the Comilla incident spread. Reports had already started coming in of communal flare-ups in other parts of Bangladesh.

'We feared tension as the Imam of the neighbourhood masjid had heard some locals talk about the Comilla incident with anger,' Munna tells us. 'We did not know till then that a Muslim miscreant had put the Quran at the feet of the Hindu god. The district board chairman of our party, Awami League, had warned everyone that no mischief should be allowed. We were told to keep vigil. We did. But that was not enough.'

We have come to Narottampur village in Chaumuhoni municipality area, Begumganj's sub-district, an hour's drive from Gandhi Ashram. It is late evening now. Inside a narrow lane, next to a pandal that is being readied for 2022 Durga Puja celebrations (which is still a month away), Mukta Das stays in a one-storied house of gloom. We do not have the heart to look her in the eye or ask her to recollect what happened here a year ago. News headlines had said that she had lost her brother, Jatan Saha to communal violence.[9]

News of outsiders coming to meet her has spread and some of her neighbours have streamed into the tiny living room, where her bedridden father-in-law is resting on a divan. Among those present in the room is Munna who now encourages her to speak to us: 'India *theke eshechen* (They have come from India).'

The next thirty minutes pass in a daze. 'My brother, Jatan had come home for pujo. The pandal is right outside the house. You must have seen it,' she begins. We nod that we have. What Mukta Das tells us next while fighting back her tears, makes it difficult for us to keep a clear head and record her testimonial. But we try.

'The Comilla incident had already happened and the local administration told us to do the visarjan of all the idols in all the pandals in the locality as soon as possible on Dasami. We did so by 10 a.m. We thought now that the pujo was over and the goddess had been immersed in water, no harm would come. How wrong we were!

'At first, it was not more than 200 men. We did not think that they had gathered here for trouble. But they came near Muchipara, which is close by, and started throwing stones at our houses. That was the beginning. They threw stones, abused us verbally and left. We had closed our doors and windows. When they came back, 200 had swelled to more than 2,000. Jatan had gone to the ISKCON temple which is in the next lane. He came face to face with these men. They attacked him with rods. He came limping back, his foot badly hurt. We begged him to stay inside the house. But my brother was not someone to hide from trouble. He went out again.' Mukta takes a pause. Tears have started flowing down her cheeks. Eyes of the men in the room are downcast. Outside, the day has given way to darkness.

'This time, the attackers didn't spare him,' she says. 'They hit him on the head and everywhere else. They left him battered outside the house. We called for an ambulance. There weren't any. We took him to a nearby hospital. He was then shifted to Begumganj [upazila] Health Complex. Doctors did what they could do. They saw no change in his condition. He was then shifted to Noakhali General Hospital. He died there.'

Researching the Partition history, documenting oral histories of women and men who survived those bloody days and months have made us somewhat callous, insensitive even, about death. We tally the toll, reduce the dead to numbers as we put pen to paper. But as Mukta relives a day from her life a year ago, our breaths get laboured. We look around the room—the men standing around us, Muslim and Hindu, their eyes downcast, the frail father-in-law on the divan, the dim light, the colour faded on the walls. We wait for Mukta to begin again.

'What do you do when 2,000 men come to your locality to attack you?' she says. 'It was not just Jatan who faced them. The boys from the locality tried to stop them with sticks and stones. But they were too many. They tried to break doors and windows of our houses. If they had managed to do that, God knows what would have happened to us. You saw the Durga pandal right outside our house? Well, the custom is that we keep this Durga idol for a year inside the pandal. We do not immerse it in water on Dasami. Last year, when they came to attack us, they also brought gunpowder with them. The one who got up and desecrated the idol of Goddess Durga with gunpowder and then set her on fire, was just a boy. He was just a boy!'

Were the men who came to attack them from this locality?

Mukta looks at Aminul Hoq Munna. 'No,' he tells us. 'Not all of them. I saw them from close quarters. When they were throwing stones near Muchipara, there were ten to twelve policemen trying to control the situation. One of the policemen asked me to help them in controlling these people. He said since I am a local leader they might see me and desist from throwing stones. But I didn't know them, neither did they know me. I got eight local Awami League members with me. We took three bikes and the officer-in-charge of the local police station got on the back seat of my bike. The crowd had split and some of them had reached the Radhamadhob Mandir. The police officer behind me on the bike feared the temple might be the next target of the mob. The crowd was swelling rapidly. To stop the crowd from getting inside the Radhamadhob Mandir premises, where there were a lot of devotees, we ordered a driver to park his bus in front of the temple to protect it. We parked our bikes in front of the bus and stood there. The mob couldn't enter the temple and started going towards the ISKCON temple. More policemen had arrived by then and we were now thirty. But the mob was 2,000 or maybe more, and they were splitting into groups, coming in from all sides, pouring into the lanes and bylanes. We knew we wouldn't be able to stop them anymore.'

Did the administration fail?

'I am a member of the party that is in government in this country. I will admit that the administration should have employed more policemen here after our distress calls. Too few policemen and too big a mob—we could not have saved Noakhali. Also, I had repeatedly requested the police officers to fire in the air to scare the mob. They didn't do that. I don't know why. Maybe they were scared,' Munna says.

'As they approached the ISKCON temple and then these lanes, their numbers swelled even more. Most were unknown faces, but I think this couldn't have been done without the help of locals. There were some miscreants among Awami League supporters as well, we would find out later. The mob knew the location of this particular pandal which is at the end of the lane. This information must have come from a local. I got down from the bike and ran towards them as they started raining down their sticks and rods on the doors of the houses. They turned towards me.'

Munna parts the hair on his skull to show us the scars. 'I fell face down on a ditch. I could have died that day.'

It is almost 6 p.m. and the priests of the ISKCON temple are tending to the throng of devotees. Head priest, Rosopriyo Das, invites us to his room. The mob had ransacked this temple last year and of the two people who were killed in Noakhali, one was a devotee of this temple. The body was found floating in the temple pond next day. 'Muslims visit ISKCON and have food with us. This temple does not discriminate. We have even allowed the huzurs to come here and read the Quran. I asked the mob why are they ransacking this place? They threw a brick at me as reply. One bhakt was hit in the head with a cleaver, another was thrashed and forced to read the Kalma (the Islamic oath of allegiance). They went inside the rooms of all our priests, the main office room, and broke everything they saw. They looted ₹12 lakh in cash, took away laptops and desktops, broke the CCTV cameras, set fire to posters of our gods. On their way out they killed that boy and threw his body in the pond.'[10]

One year after the incident, as Durga Puja approaches again does Rosopriya Das feel safer?

'If a fake news item that a Hindu has kept the Quran at the feet of Hanuman can lead to such mayhem, what hope do we have?' he says. 'Yes, only two people might have died in Noakhali in last year's violence. But look around and you will find boys and men without an arm or a leg walking around. They will remind you of what was.'

What was it like in 1946? When freedom from 200 years of British rule was becoming a reality, Bengali-Hindu women and men, in village after village in Noakhali district of undivided Bengal, the same place where we now are, were raped and killed, or forcibly converted.

Then too, it had started with fake news.

It was the time of Ghulam Sarwar Hussaini and Rajendralal Chowdhury. A prominent politician and the hereditary Pir of Daira Sharif in Noakhali, Hussaini had considerable influence in the district. So did Rajendralal Chowdhury, the president of Noakhali Bar Association. But Hussaini was prepping for a sequel to the Great Calcutta Killings of August, this time in favour of Muslims. He and his followers were setting the stage for a massacre, by giving provocative speeches in rally after rally. He called on the persecuted Bihari-Muslims who had settled in Noakhali. He created a force to provide the Biharis with security and accommodation. It was known as the 'Miyar Fauj' (Miah's Army).

In October 1946, Trayambakanand, a saint from the Bharat Sevasram Sangha, came to stay at Chowdhury's house in Karpara. Someone close to Hussaini is believed to have spread the rumor that Trayambakanand wanted to perform some dark ritual with Muslim blood. This spread unrest.

Hussaini took advantage of the rumour and announced to his supporters that he would cut off the heads of Trayambakanand and Chowdhury, and also overthrow the

Hindu zamindars of the area. On 11 October, a Muslim mob attacked Chowdhury's house. He, with his family members and neighbours, put up a courageous resistance. But not for long.

The beheading of Rajendralal Chowdhury is etched forever in Noakhali's bloodied history. Chowdhury was not the only one to fall that day. The house of Suren Basu, a landlord of Narayanpur, was also attacked. Then they turned towards the ordinary Hindus.

Two weeks after our 13 September visit to Noakhali, we make our way to Netaji Nagar Colony in Howrah, West Bengal. As we reach Belur railway station and take an auto-rickshaw through meandering lanes to reach the colony, from where the Partition history stares back at us. Residents of the colony don't have legal papers for the plots on which their houses stand; they are refugees who escaped communal violence in what was once the eastern part of undivided Bengal and settled here.

Smritikana Biswas' house is at the far end of a blind lane. Born and raised in pre-Partition Noakhali, she saw the genocide of 1946 and has lived a long life remembering what happened. Now ninety, age has confined her to the bed, but her mind meanders through the pages of history, her own and of her people, back when there was only one Bengal and one country.

'I have never been able to forget those days,' she says, 'when neighbours became rioters and friends became murderers. The stench of blood haunts me to this day. When you told me you wanted to talk about the Partition, my mind took me back to Noakhali of 1946. I was twelve. Loot, arson, stabbings were becoming the order of the day. One of my sisters was just seven months old. One day some Hindu village elders took us to the Feni College building, which was close by. We left everything back home and took refuge there. Most of the Hindus from our village had huddled there. Later, some good-hearted Muslim men came to us and asked for our house keys so that they could bring us some money and gold. The building had a security guard. I remember he would come and tell us to make sure no one made any sound, and make sure that the children remained silent. It should appear from outside that the college building was deserted. Or else, a mob could come and kill us all.

'But my seven-month-old sister cried out in hunger. We gave her some treacle to make her stop crying, but she would start wailing soon after. My father told us that we had to kill her as she simply wouldn't stop crying. And her wails would bring the mob to us. She cried and cried, till she cried no more.'

As Smritikana pauses, we do not have it in us to ask her why her sister didn't cry any more. But that reminds us of the concept of 'Flashbulb Memory'.

Roger Brown and James Kulik coined the phrase 'Flashbulb Memory' in 1977, which referred to an accurate and exceptionally vivid long-lasting memory for the circumstances surrounding learning about a dramatic event.

Detail, vividness, accuracy and resistance to forgetting were initially identified as the distinct properties of flashbulb memories. Seventy-eight years after she lived this horror, it must be Flashbulb Memory[11] that makes Smritikana Biswas bring Noakhali of 1946 alive for us.

'After we came out of the college building, we rented a house near Feni station for nearly a month,' she recalls. 'There was no food at home. My father's umbrella shop was gutted. But there were bigger scars. My parents would talk endlessly about women getting abducted. We were four sisters. One night, my father didn't return. We feared the worst. Street stabbings of Hindus were rampant. He came back the next morning. He had spent the night atop a jackfruit tree after he saw a mob coming from a distance. Had he been seen, he would have been killed. From the tree, he could see others being stabbed and houses being set on fire.'

Marianne Hirsch—William Peterfield Trent Professor Emerita of English and Comparative Literature and the Institute for the Study of Sexuality and Gender at Columbia University, who researches the transmission of memories of violence across generations—believes that the bodily, psychic and affective impact of trauma and its aftermath, the ways in which one trauma can recall or reactivate the effects of another, exceed the bounds of traditional historical archives and methodologies.[12]

From Smritikana's retelling of the past, her father's fears for the safety of his four daughters hit us. We think of the day we spent in Noakhali (just two weeks before) and say a silent prayer for the survivors we met.

Smritikana continues, 'My father had seen how women were snatched away from their families, never to be found again. Many a times the families wouldn't look for them. There was nothing to find. If they were lucky, their abductors would marry them.'

Oral retellings of 1946 Noakhali violence find their way into *The Life of Mahatma Gandhi* by American journalist and author Louis Fischer:

> Mr. Arthur Henderson told the House of Commons on November 4, 1946 that the dead people in Noakhali and contiguous Tipperah districts had not yet been counted ... Thousands of Hindu women were abducted and married to Moslems against their will ... Hindu men were compelled to grow beards, to twist their loincloths the Moslem instead of the Hindu way, and to recite the *Koran*. Stone idols were smashed and Hindu temples desecrated.[13]

Noakhali's Hindu women were the biggest victims in 1946. Muriel Lester, Gandhi's hostess during the Second Round Table Conference in England and also an international figure for peace, was shaken when she saw what happened to women.[14] She visited Noakhali and wrote:

> Worst of all was the plight of women. Several of them had to watch their husbands being murdered and then

> be forcibly converted and married to some of those responsible for their death. These women had a dead look. It was not despair. Nothing so active was there. It was blankness … the eating of beef and the declaration of allegiance to Islam has been forced upon many women as a price for their lives.[15]

The forced conversions make the 1946 Noakhali violence an interesting study. Rakesh Batabyal, a professor of History at Jawaharlal Nehru University, India, believes that the riots began with Islam and ended with Islam. In other riots, religion was the point of disagreement.[16] In Noakhali, religion was also the instrument that ended the disagreement. The attacks in Noakhali on Hindus by Muslims ended when the Hindus became Muslims.

An assembly proceeding proves this. Huseyn Shaheed Suhrawardy, the Prime Minister of Bengal (1946–47), and later and the Prime Minister of Pakistan (1956–57), said in the floor of the House that there were at least 9,895 cases of forcible conversion in Tippera. When asked about Noakhali, he couldn't give a figure but said it was in thousands as well. Suhrawardy may have under-counted.[17]

British judge Edward Skinner Simpson's report says around 22,550 conversion cases were filed in three police stations—Faridganj, Chandpur and Hajiganj. The entire populations of three villages, Gupti, Bachtali and Gobindpur, were made to forcibly convert.[18] Then Congress president, Acharya Kripalini, wrote in his report:

> Even after looting and arson and murder, the Hindus in the locality were not safe unless they embraced Islam. As a sign of their conversion they were supplied with white caps used by the Muslims of the locality. Very often these caps were new and were stamped with the map of Pakistan, with the words Pakistan Zindabad and Larke Lenge Pakistan.[19,20]

> On the Saturday morning of 12 October (1946) around 200 Muslims came to our house and threatened us if we do not convert they would kill us. To save our lives, we agreed. The Maulavi Saheb of Shahapur High School converted me, and other members of my family into Islam. Then from amongst the crowd, Maulavi Badu Mian and Mahmud Mian Patari forced us to destroy the images and photographs of all Gods and Goddesses. On 13 October, they built a mosque in front of my house and later Kudur Mian, Mujibul Hug Kerani and Khaliq Mian demanded one thousand rupees from me as contribution to the (Muslim) League.

Statistically speaking, all police stations of Noakhali in 1946 were in charge of areas that had Muslims as majority and Hindus as minority. For example, Lakkhipur police station had 40,019 Hindus and 2,21,765 Muslims, Ramganj Police station had 47,814 Hindus and 1,10,707 Muslims, Sudharam Police station had 32,724 Hindus and 1,82,736 Muslims. The total population of Noakhali in 1946 (that came under the jurisdiction of fifteen police stations) were divided into 2,93,303 Hindus and 14,32,254 Muslims.[21]

Those who managed to flee have never come back. Kolkata-based Partition scholar Sandip Bandyopadhyay quotes from an article written by Gopal Halder: 'Even after Gandhi's appeals, most of them were not ready to go back. Where more than 80 per cent are against us, they argued, how can we risk our lives on the assurances of mere 20 per cent?'[22]

How different is Noakhali in 2022 after what happened in 2021? Bangladesh is the first constitutionally secular country in South Asia, having declared itself an explicitly secular state in 1972, four years before the Preamble to the Constitution asserted that India was a secular nation with the forty-second Amendment of the Constitution of India in 1976. Bangladesh was the first and only Muslim-majority country in South Asia to have secularism in its constitution. Would all of that come to naught?

As we were leaving Noakhali, Mukta Das said, 'What you see are corpses.' Her words stay in our minds.

Durga Puja 2022 passed more or less peacefully in Bangladesh. We were back in India, saying a silent prayer for the Hindus in Bangladesh. Some of the women and men we met at Mukta Das' house and outside in Noakhali sent us Bijoya greetings. Quick exchanges told us all was well with them.

Flowers, not gunpowder, greeted Goddess Durga in 2022. Jatan Saha would have been happy.

2

HORROR IN THE COUNTRYSIDE

GODDESS DURGA DEPARTS with the bittersweet tears of her devotees while Goddess Kali lies broken into pieces on the ground. Sheikh Hasina's Awami League government made every effort to ensure the horrors of the 2021 Durga Puja violence did not come back to haunt Hindu devotees in 2022.

And then twenty-four hours after Durga Puja was over, they did.

We had spent Durga Puja 2022 in India and were mining social media and news sites to see if any violent incidents or attacks on the Hindus or Durga pandals and idols had taken place in Bangladesh. We couldn't spot any.

A month earlier, in September, travelling from Dhaka to Noakhali to Chattagram to Cox's Bazar, and then to

Barishal and Gopalgunj, we had seen for ourselves how security had been beefed up to protect Hindus during the festival time. We spoke to members of the security establishment, Durga Puja organizing committees (not just in Dhaka but in the countryside too), local politicians and members of the Hindu community, and in almost every quarter there was an assurance that the violence seen in 2021 would not recur.

But twenty-four hours after Durga Puja got over, authorities of the Kali temple in Dautiya village, Jhenaidah district found the idol smashed into smithereens and the head dumped on a road half-a-kilometer from the temple premises.[1] As we read reports of a manhunt launched to nab those who did this, Purnima Shil's analogy came back to haunt us. 'I was as pure as the goddess. They trampled on me and broke me into pieces and left me bloodied on the ground to die of shame.'

On 12 September 2022, we meet Purnima Rani Shil at the India Today Group's Bangladesh correspondent Sahidul Hasan Khokon's Dhaka office. Sahidul, an ace reporter and political analyst, has stood by Purnima like a rock in her fight for justice. On his insistence, Purnima has come to meet us.

'I never became whole again,' Purnima tells us. 'But whatever was left of me, whatever I could pick up of myself after they did what they did to me, I was brought to Dhaka. Because the countryside is full of horrors, being Hindu can become a curse at the whim of a huzoor (a Muslim religious preacher) or the poisonous whisper of a neighbour.'

What had happened to Purnima? A simple Google search with her name details the horror and scars, which she carries with her twenty-one years later. We knew what happened to Purnima before we met her. But we were not prepared to sit in front of her as she told us her story. We looked away as she began, looked down at our feet, we looked anywhere but at her eyes where the tears had dried long ago.

The immediate sequence of events that led up to this immense tragedy began with Sheikh Hasina losing power in 2001 and the BNP and Jamaat-led coalition winning the general election. Horrific post-election violence followed. Awami League supporters and members of religious minorities were the targets. As mentioned earlier, Purnima was then a twelve-year-old polling agent of the Awami League in Perba Delua, Ullahpara upazila, Sirajganj district. She had protested against the electoral malpractices by the BNP workers during the election.

For this, her home was attacked by around thirty to forty men on 8 October 2001. The twelve-year-old was not spared. 'They tore my clothes and tied my face with a gamcha [cloth towel]. I knew their voices; I could see their face in the light of their torch. They took me to a nearby field and raped me one after another until I lost consciousness,' she said without a tremor in her voice, as though talking about someone else.

In the attack, Purnima's sister lost her eyesight and her father's saloon was looted. Her family was forced to flee. Purnima came to Dhaka and members of the Awami League arranged for her treatment. She never went back to her village again.

The trial to bring her justice started after the Awami League returned to power in 2009. On 4 May 2011, eleven men were sentenced to life for their involvement in her gangrape. They were also fined one lakh Bangladeshi taka each. Six of her rapists are still in custody, but five remain on the run. Purnima was not happy with the verdict as she believed at least two of the accused, who are from her village, should have gotten death penalty.

'They could never catch those five who went into hiding after doing what they did to me. The ones who are in jail have appealed to court for mercy. Their friends and relatives call me from private numbers and abuse me. They tell me I will be raped again. Sex videos with my name are circulated. All this, when the Awami League government has come back to power!'

After she came to Dhaka, Purnima met Sheikh Hasina, then Opposition leader. Hasina asked Purnima to stay with her for her safety. She gave her money for education. 'I call her Mamoni. She did for me what my relatives didn't. She cared for me as if I was her own. She is who she is but she helped a village girl like me,' Purnima said. She became an Electronics and Telecommunications engineer and took a job. The job paid her well. But after some time, her colleagues got to know her story and she had to quit.

'Why should I blame strangers for judging me when my own family has disowned me?'

To make ends meet, she took up odd jobs, as music tutor and, later, at a TV station. Wherever she went, her story followed. Social media harassment continues till date. Purnima wants to be a member of parliament from a seat reserved for women. She is angry with Prime Minister Hasina for not making that happen for her. 'All these years, I wanted to leave Bangladesh and come to India. I wanted to study in Shantiniketan, West Bengal. Mamoni stopped me. She said my court case would be weakened if I left the country. But what did I gain? My life got derailed and I could never get back on track again. Why did I have to carry my shame for so long?'

Would it have been different if she wasn't a Hindu?

'Yes, it would have been. My religion became an added burden. Hindus in Bangladesh are in worse state than Rohingyas. Unlike them, we did not seek refuge. This is our land. Unlike them, we get no special favours. Rather, we fight daily for our bare survival.'

Dr Deblal Dakua of Pirajpur district will agree.

The good doctor must have read Taslima Nasrin's controversial book *Lajja* that was banned by the Bangladesh government immediately after its publication in 1993.[2] The BNP was then in power and Taslima got death threats from Islamic fundamentalists for writing a book like *Lajja*. If he had indeed read the book, Dr Dakua would have identified with the fictional character of the Hindu doctor Sudhamoy Dutta, who never wanted to leave his motherland for Hindu-majority India. Sudhamoy stayed back in East Bengal after 1947 and didn't think of relocating to India even during the tumultuous year of 1971. He believed as East Pakistan became Bangladesh, the land would become free from the clutches of Pakistan's religious fundamentalists. He was wrong.

Pakistani soldiers stopped him and asked his name. After a moment of hesitation, Sudhamoy replied that he was Sirajuddin Ahmed. The soldiers were not convinced. They made him strip. They said Sudhamoy was not circumcized. They took out the razor and mutilated him. He was forced to read the Kalma and drink their urine.

Sudhamoy Dutta is a figment of Taslima Nasrin's imagination.

For Dr Deblal Dakua, a respected medical practitioner from Pirajpur district, this became the reality of his life.

In 2001, Khaleda Zia'a party, the BNP, got a clear mandate in the Bangladesh general elections. On 10 October 2001, Khaleda Zia was sworn in as the Prime Minister of Bangladesh. On 11 October, Dr Dakua was passing through the local market of Dakkhinbaniyari village that fell under Nazirpur police station. It was nearly 7.30 in the evening. As he walked towards Hannan Fakir's tea stall for a cup of tea, a few young men blocked his way. Verbal and physical abuses followed. One of them told the others: 'Give me a blade. This malaun (Hindus are often derogatorily referred to as 'malauns' in Bangladesh) has voted for the Awami League. Let's make this son of a swine a true Musalman.'

The circumcision of Dr Deblal Dakua would have happened in public. He had always been a respected man in this locality. But he begged and begged more to these boys, young enough to be his sons. They finally spared him.

Dr Deblal's nightmare was not over though. As he begged them for water, one of them emptied himself in a glass and made him drink urine. 'I was not sure if I was dead or alive. I thought of my wife and children. One of the boys gave me a jolt and said they would let me go if I give them 50,000 taka.'

The doctor went to Mativanga police station in Barishal district to lodge a complaint. He got no help from the administration. As he told his story, his hands shook. Those hands had treated patients irrespective of their religion. That day, his lifelong service to society did little to save him from pain and humiliation.

Dr Deblal Dakua's story was reported by Bangladeshi newspaper *Dainik Janakantha* on 13 November 2001. The newspaper also wrote about many others. Ajay Kumar Haridasi, Khokon Chandra Mistry, Dulal Chandra Biswas, Sachin Kumar Parbat, Nani Ray and many from Mativanga village had similar tales to tell. All of them became victims after 2001 election results came out.[3] The Khaleda Zia administration did little to help them. Hindus living in the Bangladesh countryside had to either flee or live in fear of impending doom.

Dr Deblal Dakua had to sign on a blank paper and give the boys who attacked him an assurance that he would indeed arrange for 50,000 taka and hand it over to them. The local BNP MP Delowar Hussain Saidi (who also happened to be the vice president of Jamaat) said these were false allegations.

In February 2013, Delowar Hussain Saidi was sentenced to death for committing crimes against humanity during the 1971 Bangladesh Liberation War.[4] This led to the eruption of another round of violence against Hindus in Bangladesh. Activists of the Jamaat and its student wing, Islami Chhatra Shibir, attacked Hindus in different parts of the country. The Hindu properties were looted, houses burnt down, temples desecrated. The cycle of violence was repeated.

Till as recently as early 2014, armed gangs attacked minority communities in the country, mostly in the southwestern and northern districts, including Jessore, Satkhira, Thakurgaon, Panchagarh, Nilphamari, Chittagong, Kurgram, Satkhira, Lalmonirhat, Gaibandha and Dinajpur.[5] The incidents of violence, though, were not as horrific or widespread as the anti-Hindu violence of 2001. The 2001 violence is often looked at by scholars as a follow up to 1971, if seen from the prism of Hindu genocide.

On 26 November 2001, the BBC reported that in response to a petition by Ain-o-Salish Kendra, a legal rights group, a High Court in Bangladesh ordered the government to 'explain why it doesn't do more to protect the country's Hindu minority'. According *Gulf News*, the government did not pay heed to these reports and even dismissed the incidents of violence as 'lies'.[6] However, the government had to eventually set up a special committee to investigate the 'alleged harassment of Hindus',[7] and their 'reported exodus' to India.[8,9]

Not much changed on the ground.

The Horror, The Horror

The seventh Parliament headed by Bangladeshi Prime Minister Sheikh Hasina was dissolved on 13 July 2001. It had completed its designated five-year term (the first parliamentary administration to ever do so) and power was transferred to a caretaker government headed by Justice Latifur Rahman. Elections were held on 1 October 2001. It was the beginning of another round of horror for the country's Hindu population, especially in the countryside far from capital Dhaka and the notice of the foreign press. In areas like Bhola, Barishal, Faridpur, Feny and Chattagram, the whole month of October was a nightmare for Hindus. It was not just physical violence, but extortion of money and property.

Hindu women became the most obvious targets. In Chougram of Singra upazila, a group of seventeen to eighteen Muslim men got into the house of Haripada and threatened to gangrape four women of his family, as the Bangladeshi newspaper *Bangladesh Sangbad* reported on 19 November 2001.

The Hindus of Bagerhat area were so frightened that they kept the local BNP leader Salim's photograph at their doorstep. An old woman of Saira village of Bagerhat area said: 'Those who attacked us were known faces. We never imagined they could behave like this.' Almost all Hindu houses of the area had Salim's photograph placed alongside pictures of gods for all to see.[10]

Sapan Kumar, a local Hindu priest from Chilmari area, lost both arms after he was attacked by the BNP supporters. Sapan Kumar was a supporter of the Awami League. No one was arrested. In fact, the in-charge of Chilmari police station, Toffajal Hussain, admitted he was himself a BNP supporter. He advised Hindus of the Chilmari area to 'manage' the situation.[11]

Post poll, anti-Hindu violence in 2001 was so alarming that many Bangladeshi civil rights activists believe it surpassed the 1971 genocide. At a press conference at Chattagram Press Club on 6 December 2001, activists said the violence of 1971 was perpetrated on everyone fighting for the liberation of Bangladesh. But in 2001, it was the Hindus who suffered. And Hindu women suffered the most.

Famous Bangladeshi author Salam Azad penned a detailed description of the suffering of Hindu women in a village. Azad writes in his book *Ethnic Cleansing*:

> The young women of Hindu families at Chorduari (a village in the Borguna district of Barisal division) faced bestial tortures on their bodies. These girls have lost mental balance after losing human dignity. They kept their doors open and on the gate of one of the houses

> it was written 'Come and Do Whatever You Like' ... On seeing any approaching male persons, these girls would strip naked and stand still.[12]

A judicial commission found that over 200 Hindu women were raped after the 2001 parliamentary election. A report published on 16 November 2001 in the leading newspaper of Bangladesh, *The Daily Star*, confirmed this. Rape and other sexual violations of minor girls from the Hindu community, mainly in rural areas, have been continual in Bangladesh. In the conservative society of rural Bangladesh, if a girl is raped, the family is left with no choice but to migrate.[13]

Purnima Rani Shil is not the only story from that time. She is simply the most well-known.

A History of Violence

The birth of Bangladesh in 1971 came with the promise of a land free from bigotry and religious persecution. But as political instability rose, oppression of minorities followed. There have been fleeting moments of peace for Hindus in the last fifty years since the birth of Bangladesh. But after the assassination of Bangabandhu Mujibur Rahaman (Sheikh Hasina's father) and more specifically since 1978, Hindus have been victimized in Bangladesh. This is truer for rural areas than big towns like Dhaka, Chittagong, Rajshahi and Khulna.

Whether it is Ziaur Rahman's rule since 1978 or Lt Gen. Hussain Muhammad Ershad's regime, Hindus have not been able to breathe easy in Bangladesh. It was during Ershad's rule that Islam was declared to be the state religion of Bangladesh. This cheered fundamentalists and encouraged minority repression. The result was obvious.

> [...] on February 8, 1989, about 400 Muslims from the neighboring villages waged an attack on the Hindu community of the village of Sobahan, in Daudkandi, Comilla. The [Muslim] terrorists reminded them that, 'the government has declared Islam to be the state religion, and therefore you have to either convert to Islam or leave the country.' They set ablaze every Hindu household after looting, razed temples, and then gang-raped women.[14]

The violence on Hindus in October 1990 is also likely the outcome of Ershad's declaration of Islam as the state religion. Even the 1992 violence on Hindus in Bangladesh, after the demolition of Babri Masjid in India, seems to be an organized pogrom. After 1978, 1992 sticks out as an especially bleak year for the Hindus. In areas like Old Dhaka, Lalbagh and Hazaribagh, Hindu temples were burnt down. In rural areas of Bangladesh, Hindu women were raped.[15]

The situation could never improve because the Ziaur Rahman government seemingly lacked positive intent. It is clear in two administrative decisions taken immediately after these violent pogroms against Hindus in December 1992. Orders from the home ministry asked commercial banks to: (1) control withdrawal of substantial cash money by account holders belonging to the Hindu community; and (2) stop disbursement of business loans to the Hindu community in the districts adjoining the India-Bangladesh border.[16] All these factors contributed to systematic attacks on Hindus. The Hindu population of Bangladesh in 1974 was 13.5 per cent, which contracted to a meagre 10.5 per cent in 1990. By 2010, it had become 8.96 per cent.[17]

This shows the violence had a direct impact on the decline of the Hindu population.

Then there are political outfits systematically pushing for pogroms to force Hindus out of Bangladesh. The Jamaat, the rather openly fundamentalist political formation in Bangladesh, seems to play a pioneering role in this. It is important to remember here that the BNP-led four-party alliance was formed on 6 January 1999 with the Jatiya Party, the Jamaat and the Islami Oikya Jote and it was headed by Khaleda Zia as the chair. Eventually, the BNP-Jamaat alliance won a landslide victory in the 2001 parliamentary elections.

The Awami League years (1996–2001 and 2008–23) have been relatively peaceful. This is why what the world saw during the 2021 Durga Puja seemed exceptional. It wasn't. The violence had become too viral on social media for the world to ignore.

Our friend, the Hindu Rights activist Jayanta Karmakar, puts this point across rather succinctly: 'Hindus are, at the most, election tools for majority of the political parties of Bangladesh.' He points to the election manifesto of the

Jamaat, which if one takes at face value, seems to be liberal and secular. But it is an open secret in Bangladesh that the Jamaat is responsible for the larger share of anti-Hindu violence. However, its 2008 election manifesto reads: 'The aims and objects of Bangladesh Jamaat-e-Islami are economic emancipation of the people, ethnic and religious harmony, cultural enrichment, preservation of history and tradition, justice- economic, social and political, and above all to preserve and protect the freedom and sovereignty of Bangladesh.'[18]

'This, the people of Bangladesh now know is a sham,' Karmakar tells us. But he is critical of the Awami League too. The party is believed to be the only political party that stands for minority rights, but Hindus have not been completely safe even in their regime. Bangladeshi politician Mahfuzur Rahaman writes about a Hindu family of Dhaka in an article in *The Daily Star*. He knows the family. After election day in 2001, the Hindu matriarch casually asked the Muslim maid who she had voted for. The maid replied she voted for the BNP because she thought the Awami League was a Hindu party!

But, why do Hindus still suffer in Bangladesh now that the Awami League is in power? Between January and September 2016, there were more than twenty deadly attacks on minority communities, mostly Hindus. On 11 February 2016, a Hindu trader was beheaded. On 21 February a Hindu priest was murdered in the same year in Panchagarh. On 25 May a Hindu businessman of Gaibandha was murdered and the killing of a seventy-year-old Hindu priest made news in Jhenaidah on 7 June. It didn't stop there. This was followed by an attack on a Hindu temple worker on 10 June.[19] Other attacks include the murder of a Hindu tailor on 30 April outside his home, and the killing of a Hindu monastery worker on 1 July in Jhenaidah. The Awami League government has been unable to take steps to stop these sporadic attacks.

These anti-Hindu attacks were reportedly the handiwork of the Islamic State. The Islamic State or IS a militant Islamist group and former unrecognized quasi-state that has kept security agencies across the world on tenterhooks. The Bangladesh government has never acknowledged the presence of IS on its soil. So what gives?

Who is the Enemy?

After the outbreak of war between India and Pakistan in 1965, the military government of Pakistan introduced one of history's most discriminatory laws, the Enemy Property Act (EPA). Years later, the United States Commission on International Religious Freedom (USCIRF), a quasi-governmental body responsible for promoting religious freedom throughout the world, described the EPA as 'one of Pakistan's key instruments of anti-Hindu discrimination,' which was used 'selectively to seize Hindu-owned property after the 1965 Indo-Pakistan War—'.

The Enemy Property Act became Vested Property Act (VPA) when East Pakistan became Bangladesh. It is a controversial law in Bangladesh that allows the government to confiscate property from individuals it deems an enemy of the state. The VPA is a significant reason for the migration of Hindus from Bangladesh and the sharp dip in the population of Hindus in the country.

Professor Abul Barkat of the Department of Economics in Dhaka University has come up with a seminal work titled Bangladesh *Krishi-Bhumi-Jola Sangskarer Rajnoitik Orthoniti* (Political Economy for Reforms of Bangladesh's Agriculture, Land and Water Bodies).[20] Dr Barkat shows in his work that every day around 521 Hindus left the country in the years between 1971 and 1981. Around 438 Hindus moved away from the country every day between 1981 and 1991, while 767 Hindus had to leave during the period 1991 to 2001, and 674 moved away from the country in the years between 2001 to 2012.

Murder, arson, loot and rape are not the only reasons for the Hindus leaving their birthplace. Dr Barkat's research shows Hindus are being forced to leave the country unwillingly due to the VPA. His estimate says 26 lakh acres owned by Hindus were occupied by wrongful use of the VPA. This land included farmlands, ponds, households, gardens and what not. As per the 2012–13 market price this land can be valued at an estimated 6 lakh crore Bangladeshi taka. Dr Barkat shows 72 per cent of the total Hindu population was victimized under the VPA and 88 per cent faced dispossession of land during the periods of military governments from 1965–71 and from 1976–90.[21]

The beneficiaries of this forceful seizing of land have mostly been members of political parties in power in

Bangladesh. For example, members of the Awami League seem to have grabbed 44 per cent of the seized Hindu property by means of the VPA when the party was in power. On the other hand, during the BNP rule, 45 per cent of the land was occupied by BNP workers.[22]

In the run up to the 2001 election, Sheikh Hasina and her party succeeded in a drive to repeal the Act. The Vested Properties Return Act (2001) was implemented (in a session boycotted by the BNP and the Jamaat in the Opposition) in an effort to make amends to those who had lost property.

Little progress was made during the Khaleda Zia government from 2001 to 2006 in returning or compensating those who lost property. In fact, the government proposed an amendment to the act replacing the 180-day deadline with an 'indefinite period' to do so. In 2008, the Human Rights Congress for Bangladesh Minorities filed a writ before the Bangladesh Supreme Court under Article 102 of the Constitution. In 2009 (Sheikh Hasina returned to power in 2008), the Bangladesh cabinet approved the Vested Property Return (Amendment) Act 2009 for restoring property seized from minority groups within an indefinite period.

'Most of the seized property has not yet been returned. We are the enemy,' Jayanta Karmakar smiles.

3

THE DNA OF HATE

'Hare Krishna Hare Ram
Sheikh Hasina r baap er naam'
(Hare Krishna Hare Ram, that is Sheikh Hasina's father's name)

—Protesters at an anti-Sheikh Hasina rally in Dhaka, December 2022.[1]

WE DO NOT know what the home ministers of India and Bangladesh spoke about during their meeting in New Delhi on 18 November 2022. The meeting took place exactly a year and a month after the Durga Puja violence in 2021, and just a month before Bangladesh's main opposition party, the BNP, plans to hold a big anti-Sheikh Hasina government rally on 10 December 2022 in Dhaka.

In the absence of a joint press conference after the meeting of the two home ministers in Delhi, news media outlets relied on sources and reported that the issue of attacks on Hindu temples in Bangladesh was raised by India's home minister, Amit Shah.[2] As per *India Today*: 'Discussion on the fencing of the Indo-Bangladesh border also took place on the sidelines of the third "No Money for Terror Ministerial Conference on Counter-Terrorism Financing" in New Delhi earlier in the day. Both sides had productive exchanges on border management and common security-related issues.'[3]

On 18 November, we reached out to members of the delegation that has travelled to Delhi with Bangladesh Home Minister Asaduzzaman Khan for an appointment. 'Come to the hotel late evening,' we are told, 'it will be a short meeting.'

Late evening translates to 10.30 p.m., an odd time to meet the home minister of a country for an interview. As we waited outside the suite at the Taj Hotel where Asaduzzaman Khan was busy in another meeting, we wondered how to pack in a whole host of queries in the short span of time allotted to us.

Once we were ushered inside and pleasantries exchanged, we present our opening question, 'Did Amit Shah bring up the issue of temple attacks as the press reported?'

'Your media members were not in the room where we met', replied Khan, a former soldier of the Mukti Bahini who had fought the 1971 war for the creation of a secular, democratic Bangladesh. 'There was much that we discussed. If at all this issue came up, it was definitely not what the whole meeting was about.'

We still persisted. On the issue of attacks on Hindu temples, there is a fear that the largest Islamist political party in the country—the Bangladesh Jamaat-e-Islami, or the Jamaat as it is popularly known—is going from strength to strength. We pointed out that this was bad news not just for Hindus in Bangladesh, who are often the target of the Jamaat, but also for the ruling Awami League which has publicly stood for secular and democratic values. As home minister what is his view on the issue, we asked.

'Jamaat Shibir (the Jamaat camp) is opposed to the very independence of Bangladesh,' he replied. 'They gave birth to the Razakars and the Albadr Bahini (a paramilitary force composed mainly of Bihari Muslims, which operated in East Pakistan during the Bangladesh Liberation War, under the patronage of the Pakistani government). It is they who targeted and killed the intellectuals of Bangladesh. At present they are banned from participating in the politics of Bangladesh and trust me their number is getting smaller by the day.'

We did not contest his claims by referring to the news reports and analytical pieces from and about Bangladesh that point to the contrary. We asked him about the huzurs instead. Some huzurs routinely spread hate while addressing large crowds in his country. Their speeches go viral via WhatsApp and social media. How is his government addressing this problem?

'Huzurs preach religion in religious ceremonies,' Asaduzzaman Khan stresses. 'They play a role in promoting and spreading religion. However, some huzurs misinterpret religion in waj-mehfils (religious gatherings). Such huzurs have been banned and we are monitoring them closely in Bangladesh. Awami League is committed to a democratic and secular Bangladesh.'

These democratic and secular values were challenged barely two months after we met Asaduzzaman Khan, when a bunch of hardliners spoke out against the Sheikh Hasina-led government. Anti-Hindu voices were also heard. Tarique Rahman, joint convener of the Bangladesh Gono Odhikar Parishad, a new political formation in Bangladesh reportedly backed by the Jamaat and the BNP on the field, said on a social media live stream in early January: 'Scriptures of the Hindu religion do not offer any moral teaching—all the religious scriptures are porn scripts.'[4] The video went viral on social media but this was not the only video with anti-Hindu comments to come out in the winter of discontent against the Sheikh Hasina government in Bangladesh.

The fire was lit a month earlier, when the BNP, which has been out of power for fourteen long years, held a big rally at Golapbagh ground in Dhaka on 10 December 2022, where 'tens of thousands of party workers and supporters gathered in a show of strength.'

Al Jazeera reported that the rally was held days after security forces stormed the BNP headquarters: 'The protesters rallied on Saturday at the Golapbagh sports ground, where the crowd chanted "Sheikh Hasina is a vote thief" amid heightened tensions in the Bangladeshi capital. Anti-government protests have erupted across the country in recent months triggered by power cuts and fuel price hikes.'[5]

Al Jazeera also quoted the BNP spokesman Zahiruddin Swapan as saying, 'Our main demand is Sheikh Hasina resign and parliament is dissolved and let a neutral caretaker government step in to hold a free and fair election.'[6]

Sheikh Hasina rejected calls to stand down. But the rally on 10 December 2022 and the spate of hate speeches that went viral on social media ever since, have brought to the fore deep fissures in Bangladesh's society and politics, between majority Muslims and minority Hindus, and anti-Hasina forces and the current political dispensation. And this did not remain restricted to hate speeches. Bangladesh's deepening social and religious fissures spill out on to the streets as 'unidentified miscreants' vandalize fourteen idols at twelve Hindu temples under Baliadangi upazila in Bangladesh's northern Thakurgaon district on 5 February 2023. 'The temples are located at Dhantala, Paria and Charul unions in the upazila,' news reports quote Khairul Anam, officer-in-charge of Baliadangi police station.

Dhantala Union Puja Ujjapon Committee's general secretary, Jotirmoy Singh says, 'We have been offering puja in the temples for fifty years. No such incident had taken place for all these years. We demand immediate arrest of those involved in vandalism.'[7]

We happen to be in Dhaka when this news breaks and seek an appointment with Home Minister Asaduzzaman Khan and are asked to be at his official residence the following evening.

The minister's house in Dhaka's upscale Dhanmondi is easy to locate, but navigating through the swarms of policemen on duty and party workers to reach an inner room where Asaduzzaman Khan is sitting, takes time. The home minister says he has more time for us today than he did at our previous interview in Delhi and we get straight to the point. 'It is 2023. And the Awami League has been in power for fourteen straight years. Why are temples still being attacked in your country?'

Asaduzzaman Khan takes some time to ponder over our question. Then softly but firmly he says: 'My party, the Awami League, was not in power for twenty-one long years. In those twenty-one years, our values were lost, our history was distorted. Bangladesh was a not a communal country, we wanted housing for all, education and health guaranteed for all. People of all religions were to have equal rights. But the defeated forces of the Liberation War in 1971 have not retreated yet. They are active. They want to mar the spirit of the Liberation War. They are repeatedly trying to destroy religious harmony. These attacks are a part of that conspiracy. We will not tolerate this. As the home minister, I have given orders to the police force. They are in the field to catch those criminals. We will identify them and bring them to book as soon as possible. We spoke to people from the local Hindu community. Their safety has been ensured.'

We are not convinced by the home minister's answer and frame the question another way. We reiterate to the minister that his party has been in power for fourteen years. And the party says it believes in secularism. But doesn't it embarrass him that the word 'terrorism' keeps cropping up?

'Terrorism is a conspiracy hatched against our government,' he replies. 'I would say it is created or patronized to embarrass us. The masses of our country never sheltered terrorists. What the terrorists want to establish in the name of Islam is completely wrong. Islam does not support terror. We have been able to identify the terrorists and detect their nefarious designs. They try to escape abroad, go to the mountains for training, and then come back. We are able to fight them more effectively now. It is a success of the government, and we will keep fighting terror till it is eradicated.'

But such attacks do repeatedly take place. Whether the 2021 Durga Puja violence or the February 2023 attacks on Hindu temples. Bangladeshi Hindus feel they have no political voice. The Hindus make up only 8 per cent of Bangladesh's population and practically have no alternative to the Awami League. So, are they being taken for granted by Asaduzzaman Khan's party?

A trick we have learnt over the years is to save the toughest, most direct question for the last, so that even if the interviewee gets offended and ends the interview, we still have other answers to fall back on.

Asaduzzaman Khan does not end the interview. Even if he does not like the question, his face does not show it. He says: 'Our country never supports or believes in communalism. Our main mantra was to build Bangladesh with a secular spirit. The honourable Prime Minister Sheikh Hasina is working with that spirit. Our Hindu society was in this country and will always remain in this country. The government has no plan to exclude or deprive them. We have given them priority. They are in top positions, including in foundations, the secretariat and the police department. They hold positions according to merit. The Awami League loves the Hindu community. The Awami League believes in secularism, the Awami League does not believe that only Muslims will live here. That is why people of all communities give unwavering support to Sheikh Hasina and her government.'

Fissures within Fissures

Back in Kolkata after our Delhi and Dhaka visit, we meet Asad Noor—exiled Bangladeshi blogger and human rights activist—at Melbourne Café in Jodhpur Park in the southern part of Kolkata, where he currently stays and from where he vlogs and does Facebook lives almost every night to report on the country he has escaped from. 'From outside it may appear that the Sheikh Hasina government is secular and democratic, and the BNP and the Jamaat combine is the root of all evil, but there are fissures within fissures. Bangladesh's politics, like the politics of its South

Asian neighbours, is more complicated than a simple secular-communal binary,' he tells us.[8]

Noor is an advocate for freedom of expression and LGBTQIA rights, and has criticized religious fundamentalism in Bangladesh and paid a rather hefty price for it. He has been prosecuted multiple times by Bangladeshi authorities for alleged blasphemy and hurting religious sentiments, been sent to prison, and has been in exile in India since 2019.

'I try to show what mainstream news media in Bangladesh cannot,' says Noor. 'I ask questions most of our journalists back home do not, for fear of life and limb. You think religious fundamentalists are only with the Bangladesh Nationalist Party and the Jamaat? Much of the rank and file of the Awami League today is filled with people who may not speak hate but secretly endorse it. Not just the Awami League, Bangladesh society as a whole has been infected by fundamentalism.

'You wonder how Bangladesh became like this? Well, Sheikh Hasina is the longest serving Prime Minister in the history of Bangladesh, having served for a combined total of over nineteen years. On 10 January 2023, she will become the world's longest-serving female Head of Government in history. During her rule, there have been marvellous bridges and splendid buildings, the GDP has gone up, but economic disparity prevails and so does corruption. People are unhappy, and much of the country is poor and illiterate. They have lost hope from this life and hence look forward to an afterlife. And that is where peddlers of religion come in with promise of jannat and to preach hate for those who do not follow their faith. It starts from the madrasas. I went to one myself as a child growing up in rural Bangladesh and know what is taught there makes you look at people from other faiths with derision, if not direct hate. The huzurs, most of whom are very popular in Bangladesh's hinterland, routinely preach religious extremism, the waj-mehfils are most often hate gatherings and ever since Zakir Naik entered the scene, people got to know that you can dress modern and remain backward,' Noor says.

If not the Awami League who will the Hindus in Bangladesh repose faith in, we ask.

'It is true Awami League did not trade in religion,' he replies. 'But after the grenade attack on her in 2004, Sheikh Hasina realized she had to reach out to fundamentalists. Understand her politics. Hasina is perceived in Bangladesh to be close to India and India is a Hindu-majority country. To balance this, in Bangladesh she has to give a degree of free hand to Islamic hardliners.'

This is the view of one human rights activist in exile, a person who may be bitter at the government of the day for the downward spiral his life has taken. So we listen to a podcast that Asad Noor did with writer-activist Taslima Nasrin on the unstoppable rise of the religious hard right in Bangladesh.[9] For her books, Nasrin is persona non grata in her homeland Bangladesh. In the podcast she says:

> Twenty-eight years ago, then Prime Minister of Bangladesh and Sheikh Hasina's arch rival, Khaleda Zia,

> banned my book *Lajja*. *Lajja* was a fictitious tale on the lived reality of Hindus in Bangladesh. Now Sheikh Hasina has been in power, in this stint, since 2009. And Khaleda Zia is in jail. Why has Hasina not revoked the ban? Why has she not brought back the secular constitution she promised she would? Why has she not checked the growth of waj-mehfils and the spurting of madrasas that brainwash the youth of the country to become anti-women, anti-minority and anti-progress and only be blinded by hate for worshippers of "false gods"?[10]

The controversial writer does not spare the public intellectuals: 'Most of them have sent their kids abroad to study there and settle down. Who will the country belong to tomorrow? Jihadists? What will become of Bangladesh?', she asks.

As answer to her question, Asad Noor puts out a list of what has become of Bangladesh today. In September 2012, for instance, in the Cox Bazar area of Chittagong district, one Uttam Kumar Barua, a Buddhist, was alleged to have hurt religious sentiments of the majority Muslims. Buddhist houses, shops, temples were looted, set on fire. Years passed, new houses were built on the ruins of the old, new temples came up where old temples once stood. But no action was taken against men who went on a rampage. There is no trace of Uttam Kumar Barua till today.

Asad then talks about the October of 2016, when one Roshash Das, from the Nasirnagar upazila of Chittagong district, was arrested and tortured for a religious hate-spewing Facebook post. It was local Awami League leaders who created a ruckus over the post. After the interrogation and torture of Das, it came to be known that the poor guy didn't even have an account on Facebook!

In 2017, the same fate awaited Titu Ray, from Rangpur, who was arrested and tortured in jail, before it was discovered he had not posted on social media what he was being accused for!

The list is long.

'I am not surprised,' says Asad Noor. 'Isn't this routine in Bangladesh now? Yes, Sheikh Hasina is better than the others. But is that good enough? Are we supposed to look the other way as Islamists go on a rampage against Hindus and the Hasina government pay lip service to secularism? How did we get here?'

Back to Where it Began

How did Bangladesh get here?

Let us go back to how Bangladesh began.

When East Pakistan became Bangladesh, unlike Pakistan, which was built around religion, the new country was created along linguistic lines, Bengali over Urdu, and a syncretic identity over a religious one. Bangabandhu Sheikh Mujibur Rahman had famously said: 'This land is not the land of Muslims. This land is not the land of Hindus. This is everybody's land.' But as the business of being a new country began, many from erstwhile East Pakistan, who had fought against the Mukti Bahini in 1971 as officers and men of the Pakistan Army, were now allowed to return to Bangladesh and live in peace. Their family members had pleaded with Bangabandhu to forgive these men, who hailed from East Pakistan but had put the bayonet into their fellow citizens during the 1971 Liberation War.

Bangabandhu was kind hearted. He said yes.

They started trickling back, into Bangladesh. Some of them even got into the Awami League. Bangabandhu may have hoped a new land would leave behind old hate.

He was assassinated.

Hate Reborn

Ghulam Azam was born in 1922 at Birgaon village in Brahmanbaria district in Bangladesh. He got a Master's degree in Political Science from Dhaka University in 1950. He taught in Rangpur Carmichael College from 1950 to 1955 and joined the Jamaat-e-Islami in 1954. He was secretary of the party from 1957 to 1960. From 1969 till 1971, he was the 'Ameer' (Head) of Jamaat.

During the Liberation War, Ghulam Azam told his deputies and workers of the Jamaat, and its student wing Islami Chhatra Sangha, to back West Pakistan and oppose the movement for an independent Bangladesh. The Jamaat itself was but a subsidiary force under the Pakistan Army that had come to wreak havoc on the Bengalis in the East.

Azam did not limit himself to the Jamaat and its student wing Islami Chhatra Sangha. He played an active part in the formation of the Peace Committee, Razakars, Al-Badr Force, and all such branches of hate that had sprung up from within East Pakistan to collaborate with the West Pakistani occupation forces. Simply put, Ghulam Azam stood against the idea of Bangladesh.

But Bangladesh's time had come and his time was over.

Ghulam Azam left for Pakistan on 22 November 1971.

His story didn't end there. He formed a committee named Purbo Pakistan Punoruddhar Committee (Committee for the Restoration of East Pakistan) and then set out to turn global opinion against Bangladesh, especially in the Middle East. He campaigned against the recognition of Bangladesh as a sovereign state.

Interestingly, Benazir Bhutto's Pakistan was doing the same thing. Bhutto dialled China and China used its first United Nations Security Council veto to block the United Nations from admitting Bangladesh, which China saw as a breakaway province no better than Taiwan.[11]

Lahore put out a gala Islamic summit in 1974. Derecognizing Bangladesh was one of the main objectives.

Ghulam Azam had left Pakistan for London in 1973 where he had set up the head office of the Purbo Pakistan Punoruddhar Committee. He began circulating a weekly newspaper, *Sonar Bangla* (Golden Bengal), in London. The newspaper had one agenda, to write against independent Bangladesh. The Bangladesh government cancelled Azam's citizenship on 18 April 1973.

But Azam wouldn't stop. He visited Saudi Arabia in March 1975 and met King Faisal bin Abdulaziz Al Saud to campaign against Bangladesh. He told the king, 'Hindus had captured East Pakistan, Holy Qurans had been burnt, mosques had been destroyed and converted into Mandirs (prayer place) and many Muslims had been killed.'[12]

Ghulam Azam understood the power of fake news even before it became a term and he collected funds from the Middle East in the name of rebuilding mosques and madrasas.

Surprisingly, Ghulam Azam managed to come to Bangladesh on 11 August 1978 on a Pakistani passport, after the assassination of Bangabandhu. He got his citizenship back by appealing to the courts and resumed the office of 'Ameer' of the Jamaat-e-Islami (aka Jamaat). His luck finally ran out when the Bangladesh government set up the International Crimes Tribunal after the Awami League won the 2008 elections with a two-third majority. The tribunal was constituted as a domestic judicial forum to conduct trials of internationally recognized crimes like those that took place during the Liberation War. The Bangladesh Parliament had enacted the International Crimes (Tribunals) Act in 1973 itself 'to provide for the detention, prosecution and punishment of persons for genocide, crimes against humanity, war crimes and other crimes under international law, committed in the geographical territory of Bangladesh during the War of Liberation, particularly between 25 March to 16 December 1971.'[13]

Ghulam Azam became Case No. 06 and was sentenced to imprisonment for life in 2013 after his arrest in 2012.

In 2014, he died of a heart attack. But he had managed to come back and flourish in the country he had maligned globally while campaigning for its derecognition.

And he was not the only one.

Journalist Manash Ghosh, who covered the 1971 war for *The Statesman* newspaper and wrote a book titled *Bangladesh War: Report from Ground Zero,* spotted a 'gaddar', a man working for the Pakistani military to 'collect vital intelligence on the Mukti Bahini camps'.[14] But the man told Ghosh quite the opposite. Ghosh describes the incident in detail:

> During one of my return journeys to Calcutta from Chaudanga, I dropped in at a roadside dhaba (eatery) in Alamdanga where a large crowd had collected. There I met this man as I was having a meal, a 'fili-looking fellow', in flashy clothes, wearing a trendy pair of goggles with a gold chain round his neck. He sat at my table and introduced himself as Zafar Iqbal, a Bengali hero of the Dacca film industry. He told me he wanted to join the muktijuddho [war of independence] and had left the comforts of his lavish Dacca home and was heading for Calcutta. He had no place to stay and knew nobody in Calcutta. He wanted to know whether he could stay with me for a few days before he made his own arrangements. He claimed that he belonged to a highly cultured family in Dacca and his sister, Shahnaz Rahmantullah, was a famous Gazal singer.[15]

Without any background check, Ghosh brought him home and gave him financial support, thinking he was helping a prospective soldier for the war of independence. Only when real freedom fighters turned up at Ghosh's house later in search of the 'gaddar' did Ghosh realize his folly. Zafar Iqbal had disappeared by then!

Like Ghulam Azam and Zafar Iqbal, many 'enemies of the state' had infiltrated into the system, during and after the 1971 war. Ironically many of those who wanted Bangladesh to turn back the clock and become East Pakistan again, continued to live with impunity in Bangladesh.

When the war crimes trials began in 2010, the damage that had been done to the socio-political fabric of Bangladesh by the rehabilitation of men like Ghulam Azaz came to the fore. BBC's Bangladesh correspondent, Mahfuz Sadique wrote on 18 April 2015:

> By now many of those suspected Islamists had become a mainstay of the opposition bloc. Some had even been government ministers in the past. Initial optimism gave way to criticisms from Western governments and international human rights groups surrounding the robustness of the judicial process, as it was a domestic set-up. Then two years ago, a group of secular bloggers gathered at the capital's Shahbag roundabout demanding the execution of one of the convicted Islamists, after the court handed down a life sentence. It captured the imagination of thousands of urban,

> middle-class young men and women, all chanting, 'Hang the Razakars'. As their threat to the Islamists was carried live on television—the line between secular, liberal values and mob justice was blurred by pent-up nationalism. While they did get what they wanted—a sentence of death, from an appeals court—it was soon to be a case of unintended consequences.[16]

And what were those 'unintended consequences'? Sadique wrote:

> In moderate Muslim-majority Bangladesh, decades of stealthy Saudi Salafist funding for madrassas and Islamic charities has created an underclass of poor, working-class young men shifting to a more puritan and confrontational strain of the religion. Now, feeling threatened from all sides, the Islamists came out of the woodwork. One afternoon that May, hundreds and thousands of madrassa students in traditional Islamic garb and skullcaps gathered at a different Dhaka roundabout—now showing their real numbers. Their favourite war cry, 'Hang atheist bloggers'. A new battle line was drawn.[17]

Between 2013 and 2016 secularist and atheist writers, bloggers, and publishers in Bangladesh, as well as foreigners, homosexuals and Hindus, Buddhists, Christians and Shias came under attack. By 2 July 2016, a total of forty-eight people, including twenty foreign nationals, had been killed.[18] These attacks were largely blamed on extremist groups such as Ansarullah Bangla Team and Islamic State of Iraq and Syria.

One particular act of terror that shook not just Bangladesh, but most of the democratic, secular world, was the July 2016 Dhaka attack. 'On the night of 1 July 2016, at around 9.20 p.m. Bangladesh time, five militants took hostages and opened fire on the Holey Artisan Bakery in Dhaka's posh Gulshan area. The militants entered the bakery with crude bombs, machetes, pistols, and took several dozen hostages, foreigners and locals. In the immediate response, while Dhaka Metropolitan Police tried to regain control of the bakery, two police officers were shot dead by the assailants. Twenty-nine people were killed, including twenty hostages (seventeen foreigners and three locals), two police officers, five gunmen, and two bakery staff members. The Islamic State of Iraq and the Levant claimed responsibility for the incident and released photographs of the gunmen, but Bangladesh, Asaduzzaman Khan had said the perpetrators belonged to Jamaat-ul-Mujahideen.'[19]

What shook the world was not just the daring nature of the attack on this upscale, residential neighbourhood of Bangladesh's capital city that houses embassies and the who's who of the country, but the identity of the attackers. All five—Nibras Islam, Rohan Imtiaz, Meer Saameh Mubasheer, Khairul Islam and Shafiqul Islam—were in their late teens or early twenties, and had been to the best private schools and universities in Bangladesh and abroad.

Nibras Islam was known as a 'fun-loving, in and out of love, and had attended Monash University in Malaysia and returned because he didn't like it in Monash'.[20] Nibras' father was a businessman with two houses in Dhaka, and one of his uncles was a Deputy Secretary to the Bangladesh Government.

Sahidul Hasan Khokon, who covered the Gulshan attack for *India Today*, told us: 'Bangladesh has had history of violence. As a journalist, I have been on the internal security beat for a long time and covering incidents of terror attacks had hardened me as a person. But the Gulshan attack crushed me and most of those like me, who have kept the flame of a secular Bangladesh burning in our hearts. If the minds of Anglicized boys from affluent families, who have been sent to posh, private schools, and lead privileged lives, could be hacked by terror groups operating from outside the country, what hope does Bangladesh have?'

While these five terrorists were put down by Bangladesh's elite commandos, the response of the Bangladesh government in general to the mushrooming of terror has often been called into question.

In what is seen as a balancing act, the Bangladesh government has come under criticism, 'for charging and jailing some secularist bloggers (like Asad Noor) for allegedly defaming religious groups; or hurting religious sentiments of different religious groups; or urging the bloggers to flee overseas. This strategy was seen by some as pandering to hardline elements within Bangladesh's Muslim majority population.'[21]

Desperately Searching for Secularism

There are other factors. 'The lack of a clear state policy when it comes to secularism has helped accelerate the rise of fundamentalism, extremism, and anti-West sentiments in Bangladesh,' Shafi Md Mostofa, assistant professor of World Religions and Culture at Dhaka University's Faculty of Arts, wrote in 2020.[22]

> "To what extent Bangladeshis were 'secular' to begin with is a matter of considerable debate," notes Mostafa, "although by secularism in Bangladesh one means pluralism of religious faiths as opposed to more expansive definitions of the term".[23]
>
> Bangladesh declared itself a secular state with its birth in 1971. Secularism was chosen as one of the four pillars that were to guide official policy ... Bangladesh's polity could not come to a well-defined position as to what kind of state it would be ... Under Bangabandhu Sheikh Mujibur Rahman—Bangladesh's first prime minister and considered father of the nation—secularism faced an initial setback when the Education Commission of 1973 found that the majority of the country's citizens were in favor of religious education. From 1975 onward, after Bangabandhu's term in office, Bangladesh has yet to fully settle on the principles that would govern it. This has led subsequent regimes to play around with political Islam as well as secularism.

Mostofa further writes:

> The original constitution was changed in 1978 with installment of the phrase "absolute trust and faith in the Almighty Allah" by the Ziaur Rahman government in order to replace secularism as a state principle. Rahman's government also built fraternal relationships with countries in the Middle East. The military dictator who followed Rehman, Hussain Muhammad Ershad, went one step further to declare Islam as the state religion in 1988. These military regimes resorted to religion to legitimize their power, which they had usurped unconstitutionally.
>
> The subsequent democratic regimes since 1991 also followed the path of expedient politics and opportunism. These regimes also failed to ensure basic human rights, political stability, economic sustainability, and to establish transparent institutions. Rather, corruption in Bangladesh grew and the country fell behind on the Human Development Index. Cronyism became rampant.
>
> The Bangladesh Awami League once again came to power in January 2009 with the promise to restore the 1972 Constitution. They partially did so through the 15th Amendment to the constitution in 2013 but they kept Islam as the state religion. There are questions around why this was the case, and what stopped the government, still in power, from restoring the provisions of the 1972 constitution. Moreover, the

current government has acknowledged the "Qawmi Dawrah" degree (an Islamic religious qualification) to be equivalent to the Master's degree, has enacted the Digital Security Act in 2018 to prosecute those deemed to be hurting religious sentiments, started building 560 "model mosques", and corrected textbooks to fulfill demands of the 'Hefazat', a coalition of several Islamist parties.[24]

Alongside, there has been a constant pressure to regularize Urdu, the same language that was rejected in favour of Bangla when East Pakistan became Bangladesh. The process began with the constitutional amendment in 1975 that replaced the phrase 'Bengali Nationalism' with 'Bangladeshi Nationalism'. The number of madrasas kept going up as the decades passed by. Research shows between 1950 and 2008 the number of madrasas increased from 4,430 to 54,130, and 15,000 new madrasas sprung up across the country between 1991 and 2000. These include both Qawmi and Aliya madrasas. The Qawmi madrasas increased thirteen-fold and the Aliya madrasas eleven-fold in the sixty-year-span.[25]

The government controls Aliya madrasas with funding, prescribing syllabi and management. Hence, the process of modernization is in the hands of the government. The Qawmi madrasas are not regulated by the government and adopt their own syllabus which follows a predominantly religious content that greatly emphasizes Arabic, Persian and Urdu language studies. These madrasas are financed by religious and individual donations, contributions from expatriate Bangladeshis especially from Middle Eastern countries, and frequent donations from charity-based Islamic organizations.

Existing research supports the view that Aliya madrasas in Bangladesh tend to have political associations with the Jamaat. However, there is another interesting finding that reveals that students and teachers at Qawmi madrasas are also affiliated with political parties, both Islamist and otherwise.

On 18 August 2005, a report of bomb explosion was published in *The Daily Star*. The report reads: 'In an unprecedented scale of terror attacks, a banned Islamist militant group yesterday simultaneously blasted at least 459 time-bombs in 63 of 64 districts across the country.'[26]

Bangladeshi madrasas in particular drew global attention with the blasts. This series of suicide attacks even killed local judges and lawyers.

What Now?

As Bangladesh gears up for elections in January 2024, Sheikh Hasina might well win a fifth term overall and a fourth consecutive term as Prime Minister. Can Hindus in Bangladesh expect better days?

In Dhaka, we meet Nitai Roy Chowdhury, currently vice chairman of the BNP's central committee, and a former a state minister in the ministries of Education, of Youth and

Sports, and of Law, Justice and Parliamentary Affairs, and also a Hindu! The irony doesn't escape us, but we ask him about Hasina first.

The Awami League says Sheikh Hasina is the only hope for Hindus in Bangladesh. As a top leader of the Bangladesh Nationalist Party, what does he have to say, we ask.

'I can give you many examples to show that most of the anti-Hindu policies have been taken during the Awami League rule,' he replies. 'The Enemy Property Act was renamed Vested Property Act in 2013 but the intention remained the same. It is inherently anti-Hindu in nature. Across Bangladesh, Awami League leaders have misused this act and seized Hindu property. This is one example. There are many. A political discourse has been created in Bangladesh to show Hasina a secular leader. She is not. Do you have any idea that the list of Liberation War heroes in Bangladesh is filled with people who never participated in the Liberation War of 1971? Hasina must be aware of the fact that there are leaders and family members in the Awami League who played an active role in the Shanti Bahini (which fought the war in favour of West Pakistan during 1970–71). Doesn't she know her party shelters former Razakars as well? She surely does.'

What about his own party, the BNP, we want to know. Will he admit it is a communal party?

'I will tell you this. Bangladesh Nationalist Party is not a communal party and Awami League is not a secular party!' he replies.[27]

Well, that is word play. We point out that the BNP has joined hands with the Jamaat. How can Hindus possibly trust them?

'As a senior party member, I would say this was a party decision,' he says. 'My own view is it was not a good decision. Going with Jamaat did not go down well with Hindus and many open-minded people.'

Suppose it comes to power in the next elections, will the BNP uphold secular values, we ask.

'We will. We have released a twenty-seven-point memorandum. One of the most important points is "*Dharma jar jar, rastro sobar* (Religion belongs to individuals, state belongs to everyone)".'

What Nitai does not tell us, includes the Awami League government's flirtations with the Hefazat-e-Islam set up by cleric Shah Ahmad Shafi in 2010. In 2009, when the Sheikh Hasina government came up with reforms. including inheritance rights for women, the Hefazat protested and the law was watered down.

In 2021 Indian online newspaper *The Print* reported the following, drawing from episode 713 of 'Cut the Clutter', a podcast presented by *The Print*'s Editor-in-Chief Shekhar Gupta:

> In 2013, when bloggers and atheists gathered in Shahbagh Square pressing for equal rights for all genders, a secular Constitution and system of governance, they clashed with members of the Hefazat who marched their own protesters into Dhaka. This led

to clashes between Sheikh Hasina's Awami League and Hefazat and over 50 people were killed, recalled Gupta.

At the time, the Hefazat's 13-point charter included demands like reinstating faith in the Almighty in the Constitution. While Bangladesh was committed to secular principles in its Constitution after its independence, in 1972 the words 'Bismillah-Ar-Rahman-Ar-Rahim' were inserted in the Preamble by then President Zia ur Rahman. This was subsequently removed along with another small subsection that had been added to the Constitution by General Ershad when he was president in the 1980s, in the form of the Eighth Amendment, which said Islam will be the religion of the state.

The Hefazat also demanded that restrictions should be lifted on mosques and cultural programmes, capital punishment for blasphemy, etc. It wanted statues and busts removed from Bangladesh as statues promoted idolatry—except inside Hindu temples. Gupta said Sheikh Hasina pandered to the Hefazat and supported their cause to remove a Greek goddess statue in Dhaka.

Hasina's government also supported the Hefazat when they opposed the removal of the Eighth Amendment from the Constitution. "This case was in the court and the Hefazat-e-Islam led a movement against it and it does look like Sheikh Hasina government bent over backwards to accommodate it and the court then dismissed the case on a technicality," said Gupta.

In 2017, Hefazat also wanted Bangladesh to launch a jihad on Myanmar to liberate Rohingyas from Rakhine. While Shah Ahmad Shafi was not anti-Indian, Gupta said he was a conservative Islamist. His son Anas Shafi is believed to be friendly with the Sheikh Hasina government. "The Sheikh Hasina government also indulges him, which might be something that she is paying for now because in the process what has happened is that a new Jamaat-e-Islami has come up."

Gupta said it is this new conservative force, which the Sheikh Hasina government had flirted with in the past, which has become her government's own Frankenstein. 'The Hefazat-e-Islam, the force behind the current protest, are the new Islamist conservative force in Bangladesh with which Sheikh Hasina's government has flirted with at some point ... But it's a mistake that all democratic governments make in trying to control one set of extremists. They often play with the other set that looks less worse than the other (but) in the course of time, they all become Frankensteins' he said.[28]

The question is, who will rein in these Frankensteins?

II

FUSION

4

THE BURNT FOREHEAD OF JOGEN MANDAL

FADED UNDERGARMENTS ARE drying on a wire attached to the outer window, on the second floor of a house that could well do with a fresh coat of paint. Two women in nightgowns stand outside the house sharing the day's gossip. The lane on which the house stands has an open drain and a mild stench hangs in the air.

The house—22, Sultan Alam Road in the Lake Gardens area of south Kolkata—could not possibly have looked more inconsequential. A lower middle-class house in a lower middle-class neighbourhood that still bears traces of the shanty town it once was. Hardly the kind of locality where the first law and labour minister of Pakistan would live out his last years and reminisce about his dashed dream of Hindu-Muslim unity in East Pakistan, which is today Bangladesh.

We stand before the house and think what stroke of bad luck could befall a man of that stature to have lived the end of his days in a house this nondescript. Jogendranath Mandal must have had a *pora kopal*, as we say in Bengali, or burnt forehead, signifying a lifetime of bad luck.

It is late afternoon on 21 May 2022. Pre-monsoon showers have brought the summer heat down by several notches. We have had some trouble locating the house hidden within the maze of the many lanes and bylanes of Lake Gardens that has even confused Google maps. After a few rounds of passing by and passing through the same narrow lane, we finally locate 22, Sultan Alam Road, which for some unknown reason is now 64 A Sultan Alam Road. What finally lands us in front of the house with a changed postal address is the name of Bharat Chandra Adhikary, whose house this is, and who the two women in nightgowns could immediately recall as their now deceased next-door neighbour!

'Yes, I remember Jogen Mandal. He was my father's friend and he came to stay with us when I was a child. He was a kind and friendly man but we had no idea who he was. He stayed in that room,' says Dinesh Chandra Adhikary who has come out to talk to us. He points to the room with the window from which faded undergarments are hanging on a wire.

'Pora kopal', we sigh, thinking of the fall of Jogen Mandal.

Jogendranath Mandal died on 5 October 1968. Did anyone from the Centre or West Bengal government come here after that, we ask.

'No one did. The room where he stayed has undergone many changes over the years. From outside it is the same house though, except every few years we give it a fresh coat of paint,' Dinesh Adhikary tells us. 'Next year we plan to sell this house to a property developer who will turn this into a high-rise and that would be the end of its history.'

So what does history tell us about the former tenant of this house?

On 29 May 1960, Jogendranath Mandal lost the roof above his head at a more posh address—64, Southern Avenue, Calcutta. He had been living there as a sub-tenant. The Landlord-Tenant Agreement clauses of West Bengal had undergone big changes in 1959 that Mandal was unaware of. A student of law and the first law and labour minister of independent Pakistan failed to notice a change in the law that would directly affect him. He was thrown out by his landlord who didn't give two hoots about who he was, and Jogen could do nothing about it! Old friend Bharat Chandra Adhikary took him in, and 22, Sultan Alam Road became Jogendranath's last station.

Changing houses was the least of Jogen's problems. He wanted to change his station in life.

Those were days of great churn. Mandal had come to India from East Pakistan as a broken man. Arguably, the tallest Dalit politician in pre-partition East Bengal, Mandal had lost most of his followers after he chose Pakistan over

India, stood with Muhammad Ali Jinnah and became the law and labour minister. Mandal had thought Dalits and Muslims would behave like brothers in the newly-created Pakistan. They didn't, and as communal tension rose and Hindus left East Pakistan for India in large numbers, Jogendranath Mandal came to be looked at as a short-sighted leader at best and a self-serving politician at worst. 'Jogen Ali Molla'. That's what they called him, mocking his affinity towards Islamic Republic of Pakistan and its majority community.

But Mandal had not given up yet. The Dalit leader wanted a last hurrah, he wanted to steer the refugee movement in West Bengal. The United Central Refugee Council (UCRC), founded in 1950, had taken up the fight for East Pakistan's Hindu refugees who were coming to West Bengal in large numbers. Jogen found that more than helping the refugees, the organization was politically benefitting the Communist Party of India in its battle against the ruling Congress. Also, Mandal believed the UCRC spoke more for caste Hindus than the casteless.[1]

Out of favour in East Pakistan, Jogendranath wanted West Bengal to become his karmabhoomi, his battlefield. But most Dalit Hindus, who formed his political constituency, had stopped seeing Mandal as a messiah and were trying to blend into a larger Hindu narrative. Mandal hopped from one refugee camp to another in the faraway districts of Birbhum and 24 Parganas, in search of an audience and lost glory. At one such meeting at Uttartilpara camp in Birbhum, Mandal attacked the Indian

National Congress. 'It was Congress stalwarts who created this Partition ... the Congress leaders did so for the love of power.'[2]

At the same meeting, Mandal read out articles about himself published in various newspapers to convince refugees from East Pakistan that he was always in favour of a sovereign United Bengal.

But who would believe him? This was the same Jogen Mandal who had sided with Jinnah. This was the same Jogen Mandal who had told Dalit Hindus to stick with Muslims before, during and after the Partition, arguing both were victims of upper caste tyranny. In his resignation letter to Pakistan Premier Liyaquat Ali Khan in 1950, a disillusioned Jogen Mandal had written:

> The principal objectives that prompted me to work in co-operation with the Muslim League was, first that the economic interests of the Muslims in Bengal were generally identical with those of the Scheduled Castes. Muslims were mostly cultivators and labourers, and so were members of the Scheduled Castes. One section of Muslims were fishermen, so was a section of the Scheduled Castes as well, and secondly that the Scheduled Castes and the Muslims were both educationally backward.[3]

Mandal had believed this unity would last and with this firm belief, had opposed Partition. He had unflinching faith in Muslim League and scepticism about the Indian

National Congress and Hindu Mahasabha leaders even after what happened in Calcutta on 16 August 1946. Later, he accepted that this was an unpopular decision:

> The 16th day of August of that year (1946) was observed in Calcutta as 'The Direct Action Day' by the Muslim League. It resulted, as you know, in a holocaust. Hindus demanded my resignation from the League Ministry … But I remained steadfast to my policy … I cannot but gratefully acknowledge the fact that I was saved from the wrath of infuriated Hindu mobs by my Caste Hindu neighbours.[4]

A year later, India was partitioned and Pakistan was born. And Mandal became a minister in the Pakistan cabinet, still dreaming of Dalit-Muslim unity.

By 1950, Mandal's dreams had come undone. Mandal knew most upper caste Hindus had left East Bengal. Those who stayed back were mainly Dalits. But despite talks of Dalit-Muslim unity, the administration in East Bengal did little to stop the violence against the Dalits. Where was Jinnah and the vision for the upliftment of the downtrodden among Hindus? Muslim League had put out an advertisement in a newspaper in 1946: 'Muslim League *tamam kamzor jama'aton ke huq chahti hai*! (The Muslim League unequivocally demands the rights of underprivileged!)'[5]

Was that a fake promise?

Mandal's resignation letter to Liaquat Ali Khan, cited inaction of the Pakistani administration against rioters who committed atrocities against his people:

> I would like to reiterate in this connection my firm conviction that East Bengal Govt. is still following the well-planned policy of squeezing Hindus out of the Province. In my discussion with you on more than one occasion, I gave expression to this view of mine. I must say that this policy of driving out Hindus from Pakistan has succeeded completely in West Pakistan and is nearing completion in East Pakistan too.[6]

On 15 September 1950 Mandal was supposed to preside over a meeting at Mari in west Punjab. But a telegram from Calcutta told him of his son's illness. His son recovered, but Jogendranath decided to never go back to Pakistan. The Dalit Hindus, who had stayed back in East Pakistan by rejecting the Congress and India, now had no one to turn to. Who would believe this man, whose followers were dying due to violence in East Pakistan?

'That man was a villain!' Jayanta Karmakar makes a face as we ask him what he thinks about Jogendranath Mandal. From Mandal's last address in Tollygunj we have come to Flurys, Kolkata's legendary breakfast place in Park Street. It is way past breakfast time. Late evening has descended on Kolkata with a fresh bout of heavy rain. We could have postponed this meeting, but Jayanta has come to Kolkata on a holiday and we are all meeting for the first time. Jayanta is a Hindu Rights activist in Bangladesh, documenting on social media attacks on Hindus across his country as and when they happen. We ask him if that isn't a rather risky thing to do. He smiles, says nothing.

Over tea and pastries, our conversation veers towards Jogendranath Mandal. Jayanta, incidentally, comes from the same district in Bangladesh as Mandal, Barishal. His view of Mandal surprises us. 'Villain?' we ask him if it is indeed what he meant. 'Yes, he was a villain! Hindus in Bangladesh are suffering today because of that man. He led us down the garden path by talking about Dalit Hindu and Muslim unity. Many upper caste Hindus left during Partition, Dalits stayed back because he was the tall leader everyone looked up to. And what did he do? He resigned and ran away to India. We stayed back to face the music! If he is not a villain who is?'

And do most Hindus in Bangladesh today think so?

'Sadly, no,' Jayanta says and shares an anecdote with us. Three years ago, he was at a function at Jyotindranath Mandal's residence in Agailjhara upazila of Barishal district. Jyotindranath Mandal is a follower of the Ananda Marga, a cult started by one Prabhat Ranjan Sarkar in 1955. The followers of this organization attempt to find bliss through transformation of the individual and society. It has its branches in nearly 180 countries, Bangladesh being one.

At the function, Karmakar criticized Jogen Mandal. A frail old man protested loudly: 'What are you saying?' he ticked-off Karmakar. 'We survived before and after partition in this land only because of Jogendranath. You can't even imagine how badly caste Hindus treated us. He was our messiah.'

'What could I have possibly told that delusional man? Caste Hindus are not killing us today in Bangladesh. Muslims are. Not every Muslim is like that, but many are. Show me where is Dalit Hindu and Muslim unity today. Tell me why idols of our Goddess Durga were broken and burnt and thrown on streets in 2021 Durga Puja?'

A month after locating the house where Jogendranath Mandal lived his last years rather uneventfully. After meeting his vocal critic Jayanta Karmakar, we are in Barishal district of Bangladesh where Mandal's story began. There's something about discovering forgotten buildings where powerful men once lived, touring villages where they spent their boyhood. It is like sifting through dog-eared, yellowed pages of history. So much of what once was still hangs in the air. So many stories are kept alive by village elders who saw history take shape.

Moisterkandi village falls under Gour Nodi sub-district in Barishal district. No travel and tourism company from Dhaka will bring you here. Bangladesh has to lot to showcase. This sleepy hamlet that time forgot is not on that list. News has spread that two men from India have come for field research on Jogendranath Mandal. We have been in touch with Dhaka reporters who have, in turn, put us in touch with local stringers from this sub-district who are now here to receive us.

It is embarrassing to see the small crowd that has gathered to welcome us to the village. Photographs are clicked, greetings are extended and we are taken inside a one-storied brick building with a large wooden table, some chairs with posters of Jogen Mandal hanging on the wall. This building, a memorial of sorts, is all that remains of the memory of Mandal, the man who wanted Pakistan to become a land of Dalits and Muslims, an experiment that had begun from this very district.

Jogendralal Mandal was not the first big name from Barishal. The district has been home to poets and politicians. From legendary Bengali poet Jibanananda Das to Congress leader Ashwini Kumar Dutta to Abdur Rahman Biswas who became president of Bangladesh in 1991, Barishal has been a bright spot on Bangladesh's socio-political map.

But only one man has been called Barishal's Megasthenes, the Greek historian who described ancient India in much detail in his famous treatise *Indica*. Durgamohan Sen, the president of *Barishal Hitaishi*, an influential newspaper of that time, had hailed Jogendranath Mandal as the 'Megasthenes of Barishal', the man who knew Barishal like the back of his own hand and would one day write its story.[7]

Indeed, Jogendranath had showed early promise. After his matriculation from Barthi Tara Institution with letter marks in mathematics and Sanskrit, Mandal went to Brajamohan College. It was there that he met the influential National Congress leader Ashwini Kumar Dutta in 1919. There was no politician bigger than Dutta. There was no leader who could dare defeat one of Dutta's own. Mandal defeated Saral Kumar Dutta, nephew of Ashwini Kumar Dutta, president of the district committee of the Indian National Congress, on 23 January 1937. He fought as an independent candidate but he had the support of the Dalits of Barishal and the Muslims. In 1946, Mandal joined the Provincial Bengal government.[8]

Mandal was one of the five Muslim League ministers in this government. He had shaken Jinnah's hand and rejected Gandhi and Nehru, till he realized his folly and came to India.

Inside the brick house, in a room with a long table, the crowd makes us sit on a wooden bench with our backs to the wall. The village elders sit on chairs placed in front of us and the young stand behind with cameras and mobile phones, ready to record a speech, which we are expected to give. We have nothing to say! We tell them ever so politely we are here to hear then speak about Mandal and then we intend to go back and write. If it wasn't so embarrassing, it would have been amusing almost to be treated like some kind of literary heavyweights who have descended into a sleepy Bangladesh village. (Little did we know then that the local Barishal press would cover our visit on news sites!)

Amidst the din, a frail man in his sixties introduces himself as Mantulal Mandal, the only surviving member of Jogendranath's family in Bangladesh. He is the grandson of Jogendranath's elder brother. Mantulal says he is proud of his grandfather's legacy, even if it is now restricted to this village. He is part of a committee formed in loving memory of Jogendranath Mandal. The brick building where we are sitting has been built by the committee. 'The building came up fifteen years ago,' we are told. 'But this village has celebrated Jogendranath Mandal from much earlier. On his birth and death anniversaries, we have *kabigaan*. We remember him our own way.'

Jogen dreamt of Hindu-Muslim unity. Has it been successful we ask.

> I can't say it has failed completely. At least in this village, we have been living in peace. No matter what happens outside, we live in harmony. There was violence during Durga Puja in 2021 across Bangladesh. There was no tension whatsoever in our village between Hindus and Muslims. It was only because of Jogendranath Mandal that the poor scheduled caste and Muslims students could continue their studies with the governmental stipend that he started.

Men in skull caps and long beards in the crowd nod in agreement.

Bin Murtaza Abdul Sardar is one of them. He says he is part of a village committee that studies Jogendranath Mandal's life and times and that he remains an avid fan of Mahapran (Great Man) Mandal. 'Mandal was a man much ahead of his time. History has not been kind to him. But Muslims and Dalit Hindus live as brothers in this village from where he once rode his bicycle and toured the length and breadth of Barishal.'

Mantulal tells us he has never been to India. 'I have only heard stories of his political life on the other side of the border. He tried to support Dalit refugees but he died of slow poisoning. Did he not?'

What do we tell Mantulal?

Mandal's political life in West Bengal was eclipsed by the Congress and the Left. His first big setback was in 1952. Jogendranath Mandal submitted his nomination papers from the Beniapukur-Ballygunge Assembly constituency only to be defeated by the National Congress candidate Pulin Bihari Khatik.

Then the man who had infamously shaken hands with Jinnah once, and did not leave that hand even after the Great Calcutta Killings of 1946, joined the Indian National Congress! A report published in the Bengali daily *Jugantar* on 3 May 1955 quotes Jogendranath as saying he had joined the Congress to help the nation and its people and that he also believed that joining the Congress would help him secure a better life for Hindu refugees.[9] That didn't do much for him though. When elections were declared in 1957, Mandal could not secure his nomination from any assembly seat. In the by-election of 1964, Mandal submitted his nomination as an independent candidate but was defeated by Congress candidate Ramesh Chandra Mallik.

What Mantulal asked us about Jogendranath's death, possibly out of hearsay, has been of interest to historians and scholars. Those days Mandal was busy in election campaign. Mukundalal Samaddar of Helencha colony village in the Bangaon subdivision of the North 24 Parganas district in West Bengal was one of Mandal's followers. Details of Jogendranath's visit to his residence at Helencha on 4 October 1968 is mentioned in the book *Mahapran Jogendranath*, Volume VIII, Page 170, published by Choturtho Duniya. Samaddar writes Jogendranath was not feeling well that night. He told Samaddar how the followers of one of his political rivals, Apurbalal Majumdar, threatened him and told him not to submit his nomination from Bagda constituency.

Scholar Ranajit Kumar Sikdar writes in his book *Mahapran Jogendranath* (Published by Ambedkar Prakashani, 1997) that some of Apurbalal Majumdar's followers, who were previously with Jogen Mandal, offered tea to Jogen at a local tea stall. 'Immediately after Jogen Mandal felt a burning sensation in stomach,' he writes.

Jagadish Chandra Mandal, Jogendranath's only son, also wrote a similar account of his father's death.[10] Jagadish Chandra Mandal writes that he reached Bangaon station at 1.30 a.m. and went straight to Saratchandra Biswas' house. Saratchandra Biswas was Jogendranath's follower and his body was kept at Saratchandra's residence. As Jagadish Chandra looked at his father's body, it seemed there was some foul play. There was foam coming out of his mouth. The body was unusually pale and swollen.

We have read these accounts. The truth, today, would be hard to dig out. So we do not answer Mantulal Mandal's questions.

We have a long list of places to visit. So we take leave of Jogendranath Mandal's fans in this tiny village. A passage from an article written by Sadananda Biswas, an ardent follower of Jogendranath Mandal, comes to mind. Biswas writes that Jogendranath Mandal must have been inspired by poet Raicharan Biswas' poem 'Musalman', published in 1920. Biswas writes, '*Namasudra Musalman dui vai sabal/ ku buddhi ku mantranay gore dui dol/ na bujhiya maramari katakati kore/ opar bolokhoye dui vai more* ... (Dalit and Muslim are two brothers/ Under evil influence and spell they have formed two parties/ They fight each other without a cause/ and eventually die in vain).'[11]

Jogendranath Mandal died with a dashed dream, East Pakistan has become independent Bangladesh, Bangladesh premier Sheikh Hasina and Indian Prime Minister Narendra Modi are best of friends, but the lines from this poem hold true in our subcontinent till today.

5

ROOTS, SHOOTS AND SERMONS

'THE SIZE OF the Hindu population is coming down in Bangladesh but the Matuas are increasing in numbers.'

This statement would have made front page headlines in newspapers and news portals on the other side of the border in the run up to the Assembly election in the Indian state of West Bengal in May 2021. The Matua identity and the Matua vote had become mainstream political discourse with Indian Prime Minister Narendra Modi's party, the BJP, and sitting West Bengal Chief Minister Mamata Banerjee's party, the All India Trinamool Congress, trying to woo the Matuas, a sect that much of the rest of West Bengal was hardly aware of till then.

But this is September 2022 and we are in Bangladesh, in the Matua homeland—Orakandi village in Gopalganj district.

The statement at the beginning of this chapter comes from Subrata Thakur, the headman of the Matuas of this country. We have come a long way to meet him. We started well before 10 a.m. to avoid the Dhaka jam and soon enough left the high-rises, the busy streets and the bad air for the lush green fertility of rural Bangladesh, the 'Sonar Bangla', if you will, of poets and politicians.

Our first stop is Jogendranath Mandal's old house at Moisterkandi village in Barishal district (see chapter 4, 'The Burnt Forehead of Jogen Mandal'.) Orakandi is next. We have crossed the Swapner Padma Setu, Sheikh Hasina's dream project and a marvel of modern engineering, to rediscover an old shoot of the Hindu faith, the Matua sect.

It started with the line 'Harir nam e Matuara' which means 'engrossed in the name of Hari'. The word 'Matuara' became Matua as the line got chanted repeatedly by a small crowd that became a large crowd and then became an even larger crowd over the years. Chanting the name of Hari, millions, especially lower caste Hindus, became Matuas. Their origin story is on this side of the river Padma, in a tiny village in a part of the world that hadn't become Bangladesh yet.

Leaving Moisterkandi village at 12.30 p.m., we are now 50 km from Orakandi village, where Harichand and his son Guruchand began the Matua sect, a more democratic model of Hinduism, attracting more and more lower castes who were fed up of the tyranny of caste but did not want to embrace Islam. The Matua headquarters at Orkandi has been informed of our visit. Sagar Sadhu Thakur, the secretary general of Bangladesh Matua Mahasangha and a close associate of Subrata Thakur, has accompanied us from Jogendranath Mandal's village. 'You are late,' he says. 'Subrata Thakur is waiting for you at the headquarters for lunch. But you won't reach before 2.30 p.m.'

Sagar Sadhu won't lunch with us. He has somewhere else to be. He has been tasked by the Matua headquarters to accompany us midway to Orakandi. We get talking about how it is being a Matua in Bangladesh and the place of Hindus as a community in the country today.

Sagar Sadhu Thakur tells us he comes from the family of Gopal Sadhu, a lifelong devotee of Guruchand Thakur. Gopal Sadhu had helped Guruchand in making the Matua sect popular. It has been a fulfilling life being a Matua and spreading the message of Harichand and Guruchand. And what is it like being Hindu in Bangladesh? 'Hindus have been pushed to a corner in Bangladesh. This, however, is my personal opinion. I cannot speak for the whole of my community,' he says.

Sagar Sadhu gets down, asking us to come again with more time in hand. Maybe we could visit the part of Sunderbans archipelago which falls inside Bangladesh next time. He would be happy to take us boating. 'The prawns are rather tasty. You must come back for the prawns and the poetry of the land,' and he waves us goodbye.

We have another forty-five minutes of road travel to reach Orakandi. As paved roads give way to dusty lanes and bystanders become better guides than Google maps, we trudge towards the Matua headquarters, which is famously known here as Thakurbari. Orakandi's Matua Thakurbari occupies pride of place in Bangladesh. Narendra Modi had come here in 2021 and offered prayers. Unlike us, he did not have lunch though!

The Thakurbari is the most prominent housing complex in the village, the rest being mostly small brick houses and huts. There are mandirs on one side, smaller buildings that house the office and an assortment of attendants and the main residential building.

Subrata Thakur, bare-chested maybe to keep the afternoon heat at bay, is waiting for us. Our lunch is ready. He has had his as it is rather late in the afternoon. A big Bengali spread awaits us. The famed Bangladeshi hilsa, prawns from the Thakurbari pond, yellow lentil with fried fish head and sweets. The good-natured Subrata Thakur has put us at ease already and we do not mind getting finger-licking informal after emptying out our plates and letting out burps of approval!

Stomachs full, we sit down for the stories.

It feels surreal somewhat as realization dawns. This is the place from where a large chunk of Hindus all over the globe have rediscovered faith. The jury is out whether Matuas are strictly Hindus, but a Hindu sub-sect they definitely are.

'Matua dharma is for everyone. Hindus or Muslims, higher castes or lower, the Matua embraces everyone,' Subrata Thakur tells us.

Has the growing Islamization of Bangladesh affected the Matua?

Subrata Thakur avoids a straight answer but says: 'Perhaps the official data says the number of Hindus is declining in Bangladesh. Maybe the data is true. But let me tell you the followers of Matua religion are increasing with every passing day. Hindus and Matuas are becoming interchangeable.'

We mull on the statement, wondering why the growing clout of the Matuas among Hindus has not made headlines yet.

'Come let me show you around,' Subrata Thakur tells us.

Durga Puja is a month away. At one corner of Thakurbari, potters are busy giving final touches to Durga and her children. The Asura is ready. Thakurbari stands as a fine blend of Sanatan dharma and a new sect.

In the nineteenth century, the story goes that Harichand Thakur became famous in Orakandi and neighbouring villages by performing miracles. His friends spread the word that Harichand was special. With time the young miracle worker started working for society's downtrodden. Twelve of his friends spread his name far and wide. Often called by later-day Matuas as the 'Twelve Mad Men', this group told people there was a new way to get salvation, the way of Harichand Thakur, the way of the Matua.

What started off as a sect primarily for the lower caste Hindus of Eastern Bengal, soon embraced followers from the higher castes. Buddhimonto, Harichand Thakur's friend and follower, came from a Kayastha family. (In the traditional Bengali Hindu caste system, the Kayastha comes immediately after the Brahmin.) This continued even in Guruchand Thakur's time. Nogen Gosai, a close associate, was from a Kayastha family while Gangadhar Pagal, another follower, was a Brahmin. The tradition continues. Subrata Thakur tells us there are around 1.5 crore Hindus in Bangladesh. He believes nearly one crore among them are Matuas. '*Edeshe Hindu Komche, Matua barche* (The size of the Hindu population is declining in Bangladesh but Matuas are increasing in numbers),' the head of Orakandi Thakurbari says again.

'Come Wednesday, this place gets crowded. The faithful come from all corners of Bangladesh to offer prayers here.'

Why Wednesdays?

'Harichand Thakur was born on a Wednesday. People from all castes and religions come here on Wednesdays. They are all Matuas. Even Muslim women in burqas come here. That is the miracle of Harichand and Guruchand.' Subrata Thakur shows us a holy pond in the premises, the Kamana Sagar. Devotees believe the pond has mysterious powers and will grant them their wish. Big gatherings take place during Baruni Mela, the festival on the birth anniversary of Harichand Thakur. People from all corners of Bangladesh come to offer their prayers at Orakandi Thakurbari. Baruni Mela is also celebrated in

West Bengal's Thakurnagar, the Matua headquarters on the Indian side.

What makes Matuas tick?

'Harichand Thakur planted the seed of secularism in Eastern Bengal nearly 200 years ago. He aimed to build up a communion with God with a more open heart, excluding none.'

But how far can secularism take you in today's Bangladesh, we wonder.

Subrata Thakur takes time to answer us. 'Fundamentalism is on the rise everywhere. Bangladesh is no exception. Parties like the Bangladesh Nationalist Party create religious strife. But there are good forces at work as well. Sheikh Hasina is doing her bit as the Prime Minister to keep religious hatred at bay.'

Subrata Thakur is currently joint general secretary of Gopalganj district of the ruling Awami League. So we don't know if this statement came from a politician or a man of god. But as evening falls on Orakandi Thakurbari, Subrata Thakur's line rings in our ears: 'The size of the Hindu population is coming down in Bangladesh but the Matuas are increasing in numbers.'

Is that a good thing or bad?

It must be a good thing that the deep roots of Hinduism have not only grown deeper but various offshoots of the faith have thrived over time in Bangladesh. In a far corner of Chittagong district, on a rain-drenched Saturday, we go in search of one such offshoot. A long, wide outer road leads us up a hilly path to a temple complex.

We climb the stairs to enter the mystic Ram Thakur's ashram known as Kaibalya Dham. With a sprawling campus, an extended prayer hall filled to the brim with devotees chanting the name of Ram, residential quarters for monks and ashram mates and an office building, Kaibalya Dham is an abode of peace amidst commotion of the crowd. This is where the mystic Ram Thakur preached his version of the Hindu faith and long after his death his sermons thrall devotees across Bangladesh and India with ashrams devoted to him in many places. But this is where his story began.

Who was Ram Thakur? The internet will only tell you he was born on 2 February 1860 and was named Ram Chandra Chakraborty by his parents before he became a mystic, a yogi and a spiritual master and after a lifetime of spiritual pursuits, died on 1 May 1949.

At Kaibalya Dham we came to know when Lord Brahma appears in the form of living beings to heal the world and then goes back to his world after his work is done, he is known as Purna Brahma Avatar or Kumbwa Avatar or Baraha Avatar or Krishna Avatar or Sri Sri Ramthakur Avatar. Simply put, Ram Thakur was an avatar of Lord Brahma. He had conquered the elements, felt neither warm nor cold with the change of seasons, was neither man nor woman or third gender and has the power even today of blessing his devotees through his photographs.

You cannot fact-check faith. We do not even try. But as we walk out of Kaibalya Dham we marvel at the devotion of the long line of women, men and children still coming in, as well as those already inside the well-maintained ashram complex we just saw and the continuance of such Hindu sects in a country like Bangladesh where the very future of Hindus is often debated by commentators on society and politics.

Like Ram Thakur, Baba Loknath Brahmachari is also a much-revered man of God who is worshipped even centuries after his death. Considered one of the most influential gurus from the Hindu religious ecosystem, the Baradi Loknath Babar Ashram 35 km from Dhaka in Baradi, Sonargaon upazila in Narayanganj District is a must-visit for millions of worshippers across countries. Baba Loknath Brahmachari was laid to rest here.

'Whenever you are in danger, whether in war, forest, ocean or jungle, remember me. I shall save you,' Baba Loknath had told his devotees. And centuries after his death, they still believe this to be true. It is believed that Baba Loknath was born in India, not far from present-day Kolkata city and was laid to rest in Baradi, not far from Dhaka. No wonder among other saints, Baba Loknath continues to rub off the boundaries that exist between the eastern Indian state of West Bengal and sovereign Bangladesh, for his devotees who chant his name in hardship and happiness.

'My mother and my grandmother taught me to chant his name when I was a child. It has become a habit to pray to him every time I step out of the house or every time I sense any kind of hardship or danger,' Nilay Kumar Biswas, a journalism graduate from Dhaka University, tells us. 'My faith is so strong that I seek his blessing even before examinations. This one time I knew I did not fare well, but I had taken Baba Loknath's name and when the results were declared I did rather well.'

Faith is said to move mountains but we ask Nilay Kumar Biswas if he loses faith in being Hindu every time he sees or reads about attacks on Hindus in Bangladesh. 'What is faith if it is shaken by hardships? You know there are times when I walk from Swamibagh Ashram in Dhaka to Baradi Loknath Babar Ashram, a distance of almost 35 km. It is a long walk made easy by keeping Baba Loknath in my heart. At Baradi, I see Muslim men in skullcaps and Muslim women in burqas praying to Baba Loknath. He doesn't discriminate. We shouldn't also.'

Nilay Kumar Biswas tells us a syncretic culture still underlines much of Bangladesh's social life. The fact that one of the country's top YouTubers Salahuddin Sumon's most watched videos include one on the origin story of Durga Puja in Bangladesh is proof. Nilay has assisted Sumon in some of his projects that go back in time to explore Hinduism's roots. He says, 'Salahuddin Sumon is Muslim. He makes videos on history, culture, nature and travel but also old Hindu temples and customs. Millions in Bangladesh watch his videos. Many among them are Muslims. So to say syncretism is dead in Bangladesh is wrong.'

We talk to Salahuddin Sumon over the phone. Sumon says, 'It may seem strange to you, but in the dusty village I was born, Pushinda in Adamdighi upzila of Bogra district, we grew up as one,' he tells us. 'In the school I studied in, there were both Hindu students and Muslims. My family taught me to see Hindus no differently from my co-religionists. Not just Hindus, we were taught to embrace Buddhists, Christians and people of all other faiths.'

Is that why he shoots so many videos on Hindu temples in Bangladesh? 'Yes, and also due to my interest in history. Whenever I go back in time and try to dig up our past, I come across Hindu temples. I have been asked often why I am obsessed with Hindu temples. The answer is my love for history. The story of Bangladesh's temples fascinates me,' Sumon tells us.

In one of his wildly popular videos, the Bangladeshi Muslim YouTuber travels to remote Medhash Munir Ashram in Boalkhali, an upazila of Chattogram District. It is hilly terrain and after a steep climb to the Ashram, Salahuddin Sumon unearths the legend of the saint Medhash Muni and examines the claims that Bashanti Puja, the celebration of Durga Puja during spring, started from here.

So did it? Salahuddin Sumon asks Bulbulananda, the Maharaj of Medhash Munir Ashram, whether the Durga Puja began from here or from Ramrama village in Tahirpur where King Kangsha Narayana is said to have started puja rituals in 1480 AD. The Maharaj replies he is too young to know of something that old![1]

Ravaged during the Liberation War, this Ashram was once again built brick-by-brick on top of this hill to bring Medhash Muni's devotees back and keep his legend alive. Also ravaged during the 1971 war was the Ramna Kalibari in Dhaka. Located in Old Mymensingh Road, the Kalibari witnessed the bloody birth of Bangladesh. On 27 March 1971, the Pakistan Army entered the Mandir complex and killed more than 1,000 people, including Muslims who had sought refuge here. 'The purohit, Paramananda Giri, was forced to read the Kalma. Then they put bayonets in him again and again. The mandir and the Kali idol inside were blown up by dynamite,' Utpal Saha, president of Ramna Kalibari Working Committee, tells us.

We are sitting on the expansive marble floor of the temple with this forty-year-old businessman who is in charge of the temple's upkeep. Next to us is a lone woman, head bowed to touch the floor. And sitting quietly next to her are a young couple, the woman in a burqa, talking softly to each other and looking on at the goddess inside.

Utpal Saha watches us watch the couple and says: 'Hindus and Muslims both come here. Temple doors are open to all faiths. This temple is an abode not just to the goddess but also to love. Those who have faith believe the Kali idol here is jagroto, she breathes. She stands here to defeat evil and to bless those who stand with the truth. The men who blew up the temple surrendered right next to it at the Ramna Race Course.'

Since then, the temple has been gradually reconstructed.

On 17 December 2021, then Indian President Ram Nath Kovind inaugurated the reconstructed temple in Ramna. 'The historic Ramna Kali temple is a symbol of the spiritual and cultural bonding among the people of India and Bangladesh,' Kovind had said.

'And of the bond between Bangladesh's Hindus and Muslims, if I may add,' says Utpal Saha. 'The Ramna temple has witnessed the sufferings of both in the hands of religious extremism and stood again as a symbol of amity and not just religiosity.'

Near the entrance of the temple complex is a lotus pond. A group of young girls in burqas, stand on a makeshift bamboo bridge that takes you to the middle of the pond where a huge Lord Shiva idol is being built on a wooden stage. The girls are giggling and helping each other to bend and pluck lotus flowers from the pond and not fall into the water as Lord Shiva looks on. It is a sight so serene. Religious divisions, if any, are blown away gently by the wind that makes the lotus flowers sway. We stand there and think we should click a picture and post on social media, but then decide against it, and look on.

We can't stop taking pictures though, as we make our way from the small airport in Silchar, a picturesque city and the headquarters of the Cachar district of Assam, to the venue of the Silchar-Sylhet Festival 2022.

It is the first week of December 2022 but Silchar is still warm. So is the mood at the venue of the festival we have come for. Delhi-based think tank, India Foundation, has invited us to witness the celebration of cultural ties and business links between the cities of Silchar (in India), and Sylhet (in Bangladesh). The name Silchar comes from the Bengali words 'shil' and 'char', meaning 'rock' and 'shore/island' and the city has mostly Bengalis, the same language that the members of the foreign delegation speak.

The affable Rami Desai, anthropologist, theologian and distinguished fellow with India Foundation, has ensured every arrangement is made to welcome the high-powered delegation from Bangladesh that includes Bangladesh's Foreign Minister Dr A.K. Abdul Momen, and industry leaders from Sylhet.

At the sidelines of the festival, we get an opportunity to ask Dr Momen what brings him to this part of India, apart from business talks. 'I belong to the geographical region that is part of the greater Sylhet adjacent to Assam' he tells us. 'Fifty-four transboundary rivers are part of our common heritage that connects people from Silchar and Sylhet. Then there is the fusion of culture, crafts and trade ties developed over generations. Now, we want to increase our riverine connectivity through inland waterways. We are also keen to resume the bus service and direct flights between Dhaka and Guwahati and reconnect the age-old relations between the people of Assam and Sylhet.'

The BJP member of Parliament from Silchar, Dr Rajdeep Roy, says the festival seems like an old boy's reunion. 'Sylhet is the land of my forefathers. My granddad was a member of the Sylhet municipality for almost twenty-two years before we came to India after Partition. People forget easily but India was the first country to recognize Bangladesh as a separate country. Our links are civilizational, cultural, social and economic.'

Lovely Deb, famous singer from Bangladesh, who is part of the cultural section of the Bangladeshi delegation to the festival, adds, 'We are but one people. Silchar and Sylhet, Hindus and Muslims, aren't we?'

Are we? What about the attack on Durga temples in Bangladesh in 2021?

'That was not an attack on Hindus. It was an attack on humanity. When attacks were carried out across Bangladesh on Hindus, my Sylhet remained untouched by hate,' Lovely Deb says. 'The Jamaatis are against culture, against music and the arts, and yes their influence is growing, but both Muslims and Hindus in Sylhet and in Bangladesh, are rooted in the same culture, the same language. We sing the same songs. This is the land of fakirs and pirs. The Bengali mystic poet and songwriter from Sylhet, Hasan Raja, was a Hindu who converted to Islam, like many Muslims in Bangladesh. We may have different faiths but our souls are connected. Tell me how are we different?'

Sylhet may have been safe from the anti-Hindu violence during Durga Puja 2021, but as a Bangladeshi Hindu, does she ever think of leaving her country over growing Islamization? 'My roots run deep. How can I ever leave?'

Lovely Deb croons for us few lines from a song of Baul Shah Abdul Karim:

O young Hindu and Muslim brothers
Remember how we sang songs of Bauls and Ghatus?
O those days we spent together!
When it rained, we sang songs of gazi
O what colours, what attires!
What unbridled pleasure.
The songs of Bauls, the songs of the hamlets,
We hummed, O we hummed—

Night falls on Silchar as Lovely Deb's voice wafts through the air. Is anyone listening on the other side of the border?

6

LOVING THE OTHER IN BANGLADESH

LOVE COMES WITHOUT punctuations. So does hate. The flip of a coin and the story can change. And then, class, caste, colour, religion enter the story.

When young Abu Bakr met Kavita Rani, love happened. And then, the coin flipped.

> On 5 November 2022, Abu Bakr invited Kavita to his rented house to spend time. They had an argument and Bakr, in anger, strangled Kavita. So far so bad. He then separated her head from her body, hacked her hands off and threw the body parts in drain. Except the head, which for some unknown reason, he kept wrapped in polythene.

Next day, on 6 November, when Abu Bakr did not turn up for work and was not available on phone, his employer, the owner of a transport firm, sent a person to Bakr's apartment. It was locked from the outside. Seeing people looking for Bakr, his landlord informed the police. When the police came, unlocked the door and stepped inside, a woman's head wrapped in polythene greeted them. The head was found to be Kavita Rani's, daughter of one Kalipada Bachar.

On 7 November 2022, the police picked up Abu Bakr along with his live-in partner Sapna. Abu Bakr and Sapna had been together for the last four years, something Kavita Rani may or may not have known. Recently, Abu Bakr grew close to Kavita before he killed her and chopped her into pieces. The two had met five days before the murder.

After the murder, as night fell, Abu Bakr crossed the river with Sapna and left for a big city. He must have thought they would be able to hide from the police in a new place where nobody knew them. But after the recovery of Kavita Rani's body, the police launched a massive search operation. Bakr and Sapna were arrested from their hideout. Abu Bakr confessed to his crime. A nation went into shock.[1]

The case has eerie similarities to the murder of Shraddha Walkar, who was strangled and chopped into thirty-five pieces by Aaftab Ameen Poonawala in New Delhi on 18 May 2022. Like Abu Bakr and Kavita Rani, this was also the tale of a Muslim boy and a Hindu girl meeting, falling in love before the boy ended up killing the girl and hacking her into pieces. Aaftab Ameen Poonawala was picked up from Delhi on 14 November 2022, a week after Abu Bakr was arrested from the Chaurasta area under the Basan police station area of Ghazipur district in Bangladesh.

Both cases set fire to social media with the Hindu Right in India branding them love jihad, an alleged phenomenon where Muslim men lure Hindu women, often concealing their religious identity, into marrying and converting them to Islam. Love jihad is a political hot potato in India and the Aaftab Poonawala-Shraddha Walkar case dominated the headlines for weeks. In Muslim-majority Bangladesh, the Abu Bakr-Kavita Rani case sent shockwaves for the heinous nature of the crime and the demented state of mind of the young Abu Bakr. But it also brought to the fore the contentious question of the union between a Muslim and a non-Muslim in Bangladesh.

What is the fate of young lovers from different faiths who defy social norms and come together in Bangladesh? We pick up the phone and dial Rafiath Rashid Mithila. Mithila is a development worker in Bangladesh and Africa, a PhD student in Geneva and an actor in Bengali films in West Bengal and Bangladesh. As it happens, she is also a Bangladeshi Muslim married to a Bengali Hindu filmmaker from West Bengal, who has made a habit of winning the National Award for his films! Mithila and Srijit Mukhejee's marriage had become a headline event in both countries and the press of Bangladesh and West Bengal are still obsessed with the celebrity couple three years after they got together.

We ask Mithila if her now-husband's religion was ever a matter of debate for her before she decided to be with him.

'In one word, the answer is, no. But let me explain why not. I come from a certain kind of privilege. The family I was born to, the school I studied in, the reputed Viqarunnisa Noon School, the friends I had, I never grew up believing that Hindus and Muslims are different, except in their last names maybe. In Bangladesh, as you know, there are many common names between Hindus and Muslims. In my school, children from all faiths came to study and we celebrated all festivals as our own. At home, there was special focus on the arts, music, dance, theatre. Even when I grew up and learnt Hindus and Muslims prayed differently, there was never any division of the mind. My phuphi (aunt) got married to a Hindu and their son Arnob (Shayan Chowdhury Arnob, the famous Bangladeshi singer-songwriter) is my favourite cousin. Arnob's cousins, all Hindus, are also very close to me. So, in my family Hindu-Muslim union has always been considered normal. When Srijit and I decided to get married, the only concern was relocation. I had to pack up my life in Dhaka and move to India to be with him. The husband's religion didn't ever cross my mind, crossing over to India did,' Mithila tells us.

However, we mention that as she has already noted, she speaks from a position of privilege.

'Yes, I do,' she says. 'My friends and family were cool with us. My marriage became an issue for society at large.

On social media, on news portals, our religious differences were discussed ad nauseam. As expected, patriarchy reared its ugly head. If Srijit was Muslim and if I was Hindu the backlash would have been less. The hate comments I got, and still get, shook me. When I decided to get married, I was toying with the idea of staying back in Dhaka and coming to Kolkata whenever I could, and also asking Srijit to do so. We could have both carried on with our lives in Dhaka and Kolkata and flown to each other's cities whenever we could. The hate made me shift to Kolkata,' Mithila says.

Had she not anticipated the hate?

'Maybe I should have,' she replies. 'You know my daughter was asked in school why she celebrated Christmas at home. It is a Christian festival. Dhaka society has changed so much since the time I went to school. Bangladeshi theatre's power couple Ramendu Majumdar and Ferdausi Majumdar had a Hindu-Muslim love story. Her father got them married. That was in the 1970s. And in 2022 I get death threats for marrying a Hindu man! Where are we headed?'

'We are headed nowhere,' says Dr Akhil Poddar, Chief News Editor, Ekushey TV. 'I would not encourage a Hindu boy to fall in love with a Muslim girl in Bangladesh. And I speak from experience.'

It is a busy news day in Dhaka. Bangladesh's Prime Minister Sheikh Hasina is in Delhi to meet Indian Prime

Minister Narendra Modi and Dhaka is debating what the talks would achieve. Inside his cozy cabin, Dr Poddar is multitasking by briefing guests on the primetime debate soon to be telecast live from the studio, and also answering our questions. Dr Poddar is of interest to us not just for his insights into Bangladesh's society as a crack reporter in his younger days and now as the newsroom head of a prominent TV channel, but also because he happens to be a Hindu man married to a Muslim woman. And unlike Srijit and Mithila, Dr Akhil Poddar and his wife US Ananya, live in Dhaka.

In between briefing his guests and answering our queries, Dr Poddar offers us coffee. We notice an assortment of coffee beans in different jars on his desk. On his bookshelf is a book titled *Bongobondhur Shopner Bangladesh* ('Bongobondhu Shiekh Mujibur Rehman's dreamland Bangladesh') by Sheikh Fazlul Karim Selim. Dr Poddar sees us looking at the book, smiles and says: 'That dream is all that remains.'

Given his love for coffee, did love happen over caffeine?

'When love happened, coffee was an aspirational drink! I was a student of Islamic University in Kushtia and a correspondent for the *Jana Kontha* newspaper. I used to meet this senior journalist Ali Habib. Ali had a penchant for coffee. I would watch in wonder as he would call the attendant to his cabin and ask for hot water, put the coffee filter in a mug, pour the hot water over the filter until saturated, smell it and then sip the filtered coffee. He would do all of this in front of me, but he would never offer me a cup. I promised myself the day I made something of my life I would only drink coffee!'

Dr Poddar takes a pause to take a big sip from his coffee mug, then continues: 'Not being offered coffee was the least of my problems though. Before I became a student of Islamic University during 1994–95, no Hindus were allowed to study there. It was the result of the "revolution" of student leaders before me that I got the opportunity to study in that university. I was a rather fiery student leader myself and would listen to songs of the Bauls, the Fakirs and the Pirs and dream of changing the world through revolution. Little did I know revolution would come encased in love! Ananya was my junior at the university. She was popular for her poetry recitals. I had some pull in deciding names for the varsity's annual fest and quietly slipped her name in. A college senior finally introduced us and our first date was inside the empty teacher's room! Looking back, I feel had I not been a journalist I would not have been able to carry on with the affair. Friends were supportive but society wasn't. Ananya told me we couldn't get married in Kushtia. Her father was once a member of the Communist Party and he had no problem with our union, but her extended family was not too amused. And then there was the question of the larger society. We had to shift to Dhaka.'

Dr Akhil Poddar and U.S. Ananya got married under the Special Marriage Act. No one knew except his mother. Ananya had started working by then. She came out of her office, met Dr Poddar, got the marriage registered and went back to work. It was as uneventful as that. 'Or as eventful, considering the enormity of the decision we had taken,' Dr Poddar says. That was in 2007 and they continued to stay in separate flats even though they had gotten married.

In 2008, the couple moved in together. The families had come to know of their marriage by then. Dr Akhil Poddar had begun to climb Dhaka's media ladder and Kushtia, where their story began, was far away.

How is life today in Dhaka as an interfaith couple with a young son, we ask?

'We have named our son Agnisnan. It means bathed in fire. He is a student of Class VI. I see him grow and wonder whether he will be able to spend his whole life as a Hindu in Bangladesh. I am the chief news editor of this TV channel and have some agency in the city, but my son complains to my wife that sometimes our driver passes snide comments on his mixed parental background. My wife had to change jobs as she could not take the constant barbs she got for marrying a Hindu man.'

So loving the other in Bangladesh is fraught with difficulties?

'Interfaith love in today's Bangladesh is as flawed as the Special Marriage Act under which couples like us have to get married.'

In Bangladesh family laws, including laws concerning marriage, are mostly regulated by the religious laws of the concerned individual. The legal column 'Your Advocate' in *The Daily Star* newspaper explained this to a Muslim man who wanted to marry his Hindu lover:

> As your friend is Muslim, Muslim law will regulate his marriage-related issues and Hindu law will apply for the girl belonging to Hinduism. In accordance with Islamic Law, a Muslim male is permitted to marry any girl who is a follower of any Kitaab (scripturalist), e.g. Muslim, Christian, or Jew, but marriage to polytheists and idol or fire worshippers (e.g. Hindus) are not allowed under the Islamic law. As such, if they keep their respective religious beliefs, unfortunately, such marriage is not permitted within the existing legal framework of the country.[2]

Although two adults belonging to two different religions can get married under the Special Marriage Act 1872, they have to declare themselves as non-believer (atheists) before the marriage is solemnized.[3]

> When a marriage is solemnized under this Special Marriage Act, the bride and the bridegroom have to sign a Declaration which reads: 'I do not profess the Christian, Jewish, Hindu, Muslim, Parsi, Buddhist, Sikh or Jaina religion' or (as the case may be) 'I profess the Hindu, or the Buddhist, or the Sikh or the Jaina religion'. It is noteworthy that if the female partner declares that she is a Hindu, it will not be possible for her to marry a Muslim male, as the religion Islam is not mentioned in the second part of the Declaration.[4]

The issues, if any, of the Special Marriage Act did not seem to matter much to Apu Biswas because she had bigger worries. A prominent name in the Bangladeshi film industry, Apu Biswas, a Hindu, and superstar Shakib Khan's romance, secret marriage and the birth of their son Abraham Khan Joy were all shrouded in secrecy. Many of Apu's big films are with Shakib Khan, but perhaps her most dramatic performance was in Shakib Khan's absence when she landed up at a television studio with her young son to announce she was married to Shakib Khan and the child is his! Soon after, they made their divorce official on 22 February 2018.

We meet Apu at the Arabica Coffee Store in Bashundhara, an upscale residential area in Dhaka. The meeting is scheduled at 11 a.m. but then postponed to 5 p.m. After braving the infamous Dhaka traffic, when we finally land up at the coffee store, Apu lets us know she will meet us at 6 p.m.! Stars are united in their tantrums in India and Bangladesh, we think, and order ourselves lattes and pastries. Heads turn inside the coffee store when Apu finally joins us, a picture of poise and grace. She lets us know right away she has a script reading session to run to, so time for us is limited!

How is life for a successful Hindu actor in Bangladesh after marriage to a Muslim, we ask?

'I grew up in a middle-class family in Barguna district. My father had his own business venture, my mother was a homemaker and growing up I saw little division between Hindus and Muslims. When I became an actor I did not change my name to a Muslim name. Legions of my fans across Bangladesh accepted me as Apu Biswas. Shakib Khan never asked me to change my religion. My son Abraham Khan Joy has taken my ex-husband's religion and I am okay with that. I remain an ardent Hindu,' she says.

It feels someone has handed Apu Biswas lines from a film on secularism in Bangladesh and the actor just did a script reading in front of us. We do not know whether to believe her claim that Shakib Khan never asked her to change her religion, because sections of the Bangladesh press had reported that she did convert to Islam and become Apu Islam. And after the marriage with Shakib Khan fell apart, she went back to being a Hindu.[5]

So we ask her again if religion ever came between her and Shakib Khan. 'No. It was his career and not religion that came between us. He only ever cared about his own career and not his family.'

Okay, and what does Apu Biswas, a successful Hindu actor in Muslim-majority Bangladesh have to say about Hindu-Muslim love in the country?

'I would choose to avoid this question,' she says before bringing the interview to a close.

Apu Biswas, like most famous actors, may have her reasons to remain tight-lipped about the issue of loving the Other in Bangladesh, but it does remain a contentious issue.

In 2020, a legal notice went to the producer, director and main actors of the TV drama *Bijoya*, which was about to release during Durga Puja that year. Lawyer and

Hindu activist Suman Rai had sent the notice alleging the show promoted communal disharmony, conversion and extramarital affairs between Hindu women and Muslim men.[6] Director Abu Hayat Mahmud Bhuiyan put up a long post on Facebook saying that as a director it was his job to put on screen a diverse range of stories and characters. When he worked on a project of this scale at least thirty to forty people were on set for a whole range of jobs, including acting, lights, camera, makeup and transport. The people who worked in these departments came from all religions and worked together as family. That was the beauty of Bangladesh, he said.

Bhuiyan's post was widely shared and commented on, but two years later, around the same time, when twenty-six-year-old Sajuna Akhtar Nishu from Hathazari, an upazila of Chattogram District, fell for twenty-one-year-old Shayan Nath, they had to elope. The incident raised the hackles of their families and also the moral police in the region because it was reported that Sajuna Akhtar Nishu had also converted to Hinduism to be with her lover. The priest who solemnized their marriage later told the police he had no idea she was Muslim. A massive search operation was launched but the couple had simply vanished to some La La Land.[7]

Our friend, the Hindu Rights activist Jayanta Karmakar (you read about him in chapter 4, 'The Burnt Forehead of Jogen Mandal'), tells us that Sajuna Akhtar Nishu's story is not an outlier. Many Hindu-Muslim couples in Bangladesh's hinterlands simply elope to villages or cities far away from home to start new lives, often with new names and identities. 'It is simply too much to deal with. Family, society, religious leaders, how many people will you answer to, how much can you cope. In the big cities, perhaps, life for such couples is relatively easier, if not rosy,' Karmakar says.

All this has not been able to stop thirty-one-year-old Ruplekha Raha (name changed to protect identity) from falling in love with a Muslim boy from Dhaka. Ruplekha tells us she will willingly convert to Islam to marry her Muslim boyfriend as she loves the tehzeeb (culture) and lihaaz (consideration) that comes with his faith. 'My parents may not be happy about this. But so what! I will happily convert to be with the man I love. I don't see it as a compromise,' she says.

Punctuations put in by society and religion can prevent interfaith love.

Rafiath Rashid Mithila sums it up succinctly, 'And they shouldn't. Why can't we love who we want? My work takes me to different parts of the world. Everywhere you see hardening of religious identities. Bangladesh has been so focused on its economics that somewhere we have moved away from development of the mind. Rapes, gender-based violence, other-ing of minorities have been on the rise. How can love without boundaries not get affected.'

Above: Deep Halder interviewing Smritikana Biswas (89), a survivor of 1946 Noakhali Riots.

(Photo by Mousumi Sarkar)

Below: Deep Halder with President Mohammad Shahabuddin Chuppu, who recounted the horrors of 2001 anti-Hindu violence after the Bangladesh Nationalist Party came to power.

(Photo by Sahidul Hasan Kokhon)

Above: Deep Halder interviewing Bangladesh Home Minister Asaduzzaman Khan on protection of Hindu minorities in Bangladesh.
(Photo by Sahidul Hasan Kokhon)

Below: Bangladesh Nationalist Party's vice chairman of central committee, Nitai Roy Chowdhury and his daughter, Nipun, have punched holes in the secular arguments of the Awami League government.

Above: Avishek Biswas with Mukta Saha, whose brother was killed in front of her eyes during the 2021 Durga Puja violence in Noakhali.
(Photo by Sahidul Hasan Kokhon)

Below: The house of Gopal Mukherjee, aka Gopal Patha, who led the Hindu resistance in Calcutta (now Kolkata) against marauding Muslim mobs during the Calcutta Great Killings in 1946 (the same year as Noakhali riots).

সেই লোমহর্ষক ঘটনার কথা মনে হলে ডাক্তার দেবলালের সারা মুখ এখনও আতঙ্কে কুঁকড়ে ওঠে

ডাক্তার দেবলাল

ভ্রাম্যমাণ প্রতিনিধি, পিরোজপুর থেকে ফিরে ॥ বর্বরোচিত লোমহর্ষক সেই ঘটনার কথা মনে হলে ডাক্তার দেবলালের সারা মুখ এখনও কুঁকড়ে যায় ভয়ে। সন্ত্রস্ত চোখে তিনি তাকান চারপাশে। একা একা বিড়বিড় করে বলেন, আমি এখন কি করব, কে আমার প্রাণ রক্ষা করবে! ডাক্তার দেবলালের ভীতির কারণটি জানেন পিরোজপুর, নাজিরপুরের অনেক মানুষ। প্রশাসনের লোকজনও জানেন। নৌকায় ভোট দেবার অপরাধে দেবলালকে জোর করে ধরে মধ্যযুগীয় কায়দায় বিশেষ অঙ্গের অগ্রভাগ কেটে ধর্মান্তরিত করতে ব্লেড হাতে শাসিয়েছে জোটের নামধারী সন্ত্রাসীরা। কোন রকমে তাঁর তাৎক্ষণিক জীবন রক্ষা হলেও এখনও চাঁদার দাবিতে গরিব এই পল্লী চিকিৎসককে তাড়িয়ে বেড়াচ্ছে হিংস্র হায়েনার দল। পঞ্চাশ হাজার টাকা চাঁদা ধরা হয়েছে তাঁর জীবনের মূল্য হিসাবে। যে দাবি মেটানোর সামর্থ্য তাঁর নেই। জীবন নিরাপত্তা রক্ষায় তিনি প্রশাসনের সঙ্গে নিয়মিত যোগাযোগ রাখছেন। প্রশাসন তাঁকে অভয় দিয়ে শক্ত থাকার পরামর্শ দিয়েছে। উল্লেখ্য, জামায়াত নেতা দেলোয়ার হোসেন

(২- পৃষ্ঠা ৪-এর কঃ দেখুন)

উল্লাপাড়ায় বিএনপি সন্ত্রাসীদের নির্যাতনের শিকার এক শীল পরিবারের কাহিনী

আমি এখন মুখ দেখাবো কি করে?

কাগজ প্রতিবেদক : মা এবং মেয়ে দুজনই তাকিয়ে ছিলেন শূন্য চোখে। বাবা এবং ভাইও উপস্থিত ছিলেন সেখানে। তারা এক কাপড়ে ঘরবাড়ি ছেড়ে আসতে বাধ্য হয়েছেন। সহায়সম্বল সব কিছুই তাদের লুট হয়ে গেছে।

কিন্তু এই সব হারানোর কাহিনী শুনতে গিয়েও সংবাদ সম্মেলনের যে চিরাচরিত কোলাহল তা স্তব্ধ হয়ে যায় এক তরুণীকে ঘিরে। সিরাজগঞ্জ জেলার উল্লাপাড়ার দেউলা গ্রামে সর্বস্ব লুটে নেওয়ার ঐ তাণ্ডবের মধ্যে নবম শ্রেণীর ছাত্রী এ মেয়েটি গত ৮ অক্টোবর বিএনপি সন্ত্রাসীদের অকথ্য শারীরিক নির্যাতনের শিকার হয়েছে। তার নাম পূর্ণিমা। নির্যাতিত হলেও সে তার সুন্দর নামটি গোপন করতে চায় না, সে চায় বিচার। তার ওপর নির্যাতনের সময় তার মা বাধা দেওয়াতে তাকেও বেধড়ক পিটিয়ে অজ্ঞান করে ফেলে সন্ত্রাসীরা। এখনো আঘাতের চিহ্ন মা বাসনা রানীর সারা শরীরে দগদগ করছে। সর্বস্ব হারানো এ পরিবারটি তাদের গ্রামের বাড়িতে ফিরতে পারছে না সন্ত্রাসীদের হুমকির কারণে।

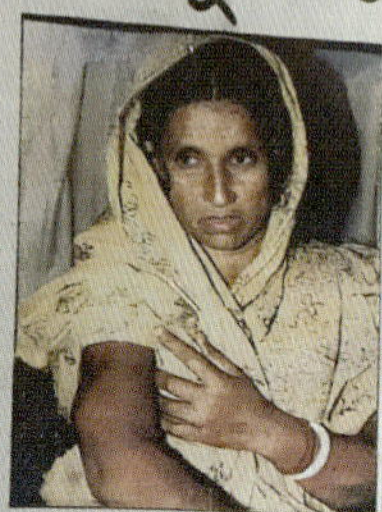

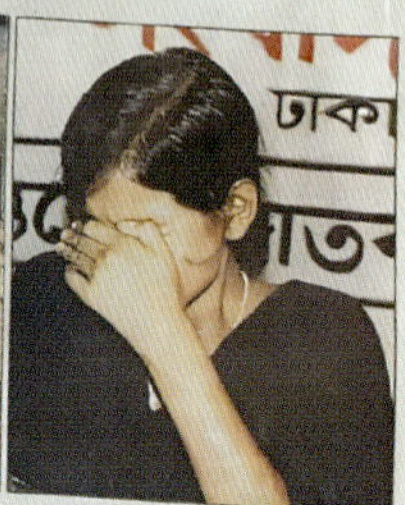

মা বাসনা রানী শীলের হাত প্রচণ্ড আঘাতে এখনো ফুলে আছে (বাঁয়ে)। ডানে সাংবাদিকদের সামনে কান্নায় ভেঙে পড়ে পূর্ণিমা শীল -ভোরের কাগজ

সারা দেশে নির্বাচনোত্তর সাম্প্রদায়িক সন্ত্রাসের এ খণ্ড চিত্র সংবাদ সম্মেলনে তুলে ধরে একাত্তরের ঘাতক দালাল নির্মূল কমিটি। গতকাল শনিবার স্থানীয় এক হোটেলে আয়োজিত সংবাদ সম্মেলনে গ্রামের বাড়ি ছেড়ে সিরাজগঞ্জের উল্লাপাড়া থানা সদরে আশ্রয় নেওয়া এ পরিবারটিকে উপস্থাপন করেন তারা।

সংবাদ সম্মেলনে লিখিত বক্তব্যে শাহরিয়ার কবির বলেন, সংবাদপত্রের কারণে দেশবাসী জানতে পারছে সংখ্যালঘুদের ওপর সাম্প্রদায়িক সন্ত্রাসের ভয়াবহ ঘটনা। কিন্তু পত্রিকায় যা আসছে তা প্রকৃত ঘটনার ক্ষুদ্র অংশ মাত্র। তিনি বলেন, সারা দেশে একজন হিন্দুও পাইনি যিনি বলছেন আওয়ামী লীগের কর্মীদের হাতে নির্যাতিত হয়েছেন। যদিও হিন্দুরা বিএনপি, জাতীয় পার্টি ও অন্যান্য দলকেও ভোট দেয়। সংখ্যালঘু হওয়ার কারণে তারা পরিণত হয়েছেন একটি প্রান্তিক জনগোষ্ঠীতে, আক্রান্ত হলেও যাদের প্রতিবাদ করার সাহস নেই।

তিনি তুলে ধরেন নির্বাচনোত্তর সিরাজগঞ্জের চিত্র। সেখানে হিন্দুদের ওপর মারধর, লুটপাটতো হয়েছেই। এখন চাপ দেওয়া হচ্ছে সাড়ম্বরে দুর্গা পূজা করার জন্য। তিনি বলেন, শুধু গ্রামেই নয়, শহরাঞ্চলেও চলছে সংখ্যালঘুদের ওপর নীরব সন্ত্রাস।

0 6 JUN 2007

10,000 fear eviction

SPECIAL CORRESPONDENT

Over 10,000 Hindus in one of the largest Hindu enclaves in the city at Chakuli, in Mirpur-12 are living in gnawing fear of losing their ancestral homesteads and an age-old temple as the Cantonment Board authorities put a claim on the land.

Officials with bulldozers yesterday reached the place to demolish the village but called off the operation due to rain, locals said. Residents there said they could produce all documents to prove that they have inherited the land from their ancestors.

"We have lived here for generations, if there is a proper land acquisition by the government we shall definitely respect that decision, but what is happening here today [Tuesday] does not have any legal basis whatsoever," said Narayan Sarkar, a carpenter by profession, living on a small piece of land he said he inherited from his forefathers.

"The crowd of worried men and ... case against the government," said a visibly shaken Sudhir Chandra Sarkar, president of the Durga temple committee and a community leader, showing copies of relevant documents.

The entire process of acquiring the area for extending Dhaka Cantonment was started again in 1973 under "confidentiality", residents said. The community of Chakuli was kept completely in the dark as the Ministry of Land allocated twenty acres of land to the Ministry of Defence in 1992. The Deputy Commissioner's (DC) Office in Dhaka, based on the 1992 allocation, prepared a handover note and handed over the land to the cantonment board.

"There was no notice, no communication whatsoever from the DC office, we only learnt about the handover years later in 2000 when cantonment personnel put a claim on our homes," said Sarkar.

"At present, there is an injunction from the High Court and a status quo order on our village, but the army does not want to look at

Above: Bangladeshi newspaper *Dainik Janakantha*'s report (published on 13 November 2001) about the attack on Hindu Dr Deblal Dakua during the 2001 anti-Hindu violence after the Bangladesh Nationalist Party came to power.

Middle: Bangladeshi newspaper *Vorer Barta*'s report (published on 21 October 2001) about the gangrape of Hindu Awami League worker Poornima Rani Shil during the 2001 post-poll violence after the Bangladesh Nationalist Party came to power.

Below: Bangladeshi English newspaper *Daily Star*'s report (published on 6 June 2007) on the fear of eviction of 10,000 minorities during a period of political unrest.

Above: The house in south Kolkata where Pakistan's first law minister, Jogendranath Mandal, spent his last years after coming back from East Pakistan as a disillusioned man.

(Photo by Avishek Biswas)

Below: A small farm, which is the only remaining bit of the house where Pakistan's first law minister, Jogendranath Mandal spent his childhood years.

(Photo by Avishek Biswas)

An old Kali Temple in Magura district where a Hindu woman devotee is seen praying as two Muslim men comfortably sit on the stair. This represents the syncretic culture that keeps the spirit of Bangladesh alive.

(Photo by Nishant Azad)

LATE MORNING EDITION

REGD. No. C 58

103 YEARS OF SERVICE

AMRITA BAZAR PATRIKA

CALCUTTA FRIDAY APRIL 2, 1971 — EDITOR — TUSHAR KANTI GHOSH — CHAITRA 19, 1377 — 20 PAISE

PAK ARMY'S INHUMAN TORTURE

Starts total war on Bangla Desh

AGARTALA, APRIL 1—Unprecedented in the history of civilization, West Pakistani military barbarism reached its climax today when the Martial Law authorities launched an all-out Army-Navy-Air Force offensive against the almost unarmed freedom fighters of Bangla Desh and succeeded in bringing under their control the capital city of Dacca and the cantonment of Comilla after indulging in mass murder of even civilian people, authoritative reports pouring in from across the border said.

The West Pakistani army seemed to have plunged into a total war in which civilians were also being strafed and shot without mercy. In their hysteric frenzy, the armymen were also not sparing women and children.

State aid body

400 GIRLS KILLED

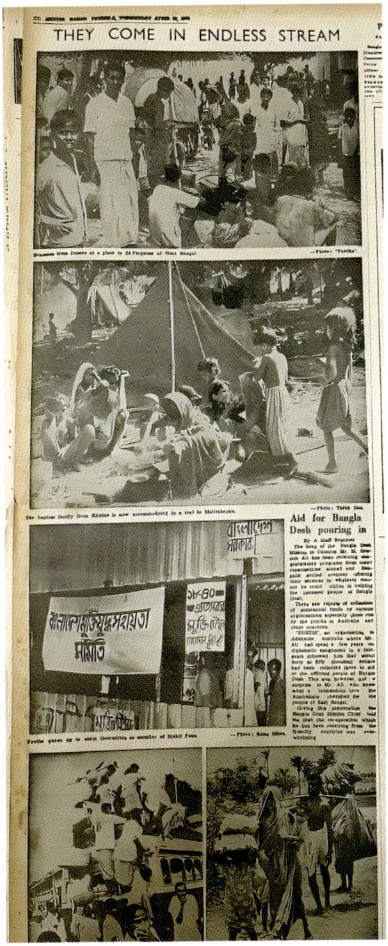

THEY COME IN ENDLESS STREAM

Aid for Bangla Desh pouring in

Above: West Bengal-based English newspaper *Amrita Bazar Patrika*'s front-page lead story (published on 2 April 1971) on Pakistan Army's inhuman torture on the Hindu minority and Muslims during 1971.

Below: West Bengal-based English newspaper *Amrita Bazar Patrika*'s picture report on the endless stream of mostly Hindu refugees streaming into West Bengal from East Pakistan during the 1971 Liberation War.

AMRITA BAZAR PATRIKA

CALCUTTA SATURDAY MARCH 27, 1971 EDITOR — TUSHAR KANTI GHOSH CHAITRA 13, 1377 20 PAISE

Mujib proclaims independence

Bridges blown up: Rly. lines uprooted Army cracks down: Heavy casualties

NEW DELHI, March 26—A 'Sovereign Independent People's Republic of Bangla Desh' proclaimed by Sheikh Mujibur Rehman today was in the thick of a civil war. Heavy fighting was going on in Dacca, Chittagong, Sylhet, Comilla and other towns, according to reporters from across the border. Casualties were believed to be heavy.

The dramatic events leading up to a unilateral declaration of Independence by Mr. Rehman followed in quick succession with President Yahya Khan's unannounced departure from Dacca at midnight last night without conceding the demands made by Mr. Rehman's Awami League.

NEW MARTIAL LAW ORDERS

MUJIB GOES UNDERGROUND

CIVIL WAR IN EAST PAKISTAN

THE SUNDAY AMRITA BAZAR PATRIKA

103 YEARS OF SERVICE

CALCUTTA SUNDAY APRIL 18, 1971. EDITOR — TUSHAR KANTI GHOSH BAISAKH 4, 1378 20 PAISE

BANGLA REPUBLIC IS BORN

Historic proclamation at Mujibnagar

IMMEDIATE RECOGNITION, AID APPEAL TO WORLD NATIONS

Mujibnagar (Bangla Desh), April 17: The revolutionary government that came into being in Bangla Desh on April 10 last made its first public appearance on Saturday at Mujibnagar, the provisional capital in Kushtia district. The acting President Syed Nazrul Islam along with his Prime Minister Tajuddin Ahmed and his other Cabinet colleagues in a solemn ceremony ratified the Declaration of Independence and proclaimed the new-born State a sovereign republic seeking world opinion in its favour to stand up to West Pakistan Army.

By ASHIM SEN

India blamed for rains

Pak atrocities in Rajshahi, Sylhet

Above: West Bengal-based English newspaper *Amrita Bazar Patrika*'s front-page lead story (published on 27 March 1971) on Sheikh Mujibur Rahman declaring the Independence of Bangladesh in March 1971.

Below: West Bengal-based newspaper *Amrita Bazar Patrika*'s front page (published on 18 April 1971) on the birth of Bangladesh.

III

FORECAST

7

1971 HAS NOT ENDED

RAVI SHANKAR'S SITAR wept.

Music became melancholia and the maestro remained deeply troubled. At a dinner party in early 1971, he laid bare his mind to close friend George Harrison. Shankar and ex-Beatle Harrison were working on the film *Raga: A Journey into the Soul of India* (1971). Shankar pulled out news articles and magazine cuttings to show his friend why his mind was in tatters. Harrison felt Ravi Shankar's pain.

By the end of June 1971, Harrison got busy with organizing a music concert to raise funds and let the world know what Ravi Shankar was so distressed about. The venue for the event was New York's iconic Madison Square Garden. A star-studded crew was put together to perform. Shankar and Harrison told everyone the concert was not political, but blame games started. President Richard Nixon and Secretary of State Henry Kissinger were angry with the duo. 'Goddamn Indians!' a furious Nixon reportedly said in a private chat on funds pouring in for the concert.[1]

On 1 August 1971, two concerts were held at Madison Square Garden—at 2.30 p.m. and 8 p.m. The Indian section, included Ravi Shankar, Ali Akbar Khan, Alla Rakha and Kamala Chakravarty among others; the Western section was made up of George Harrison, Ringo Starr, Eric Clapton, Bob Dylan, Billy Preston, Leon Russell and the band Badfinger.

The audience was more than 40,000-strong and close to US$ 250,000 was raised. This was followed by a live album and a live concert documentary by Apple Films. The proceeds from the concert were handed over to UNICEF. The money went to give relief to a newborn—a new nation birthed from the massacre of millions. Many of them Bengali Hindus, who were ravaged, raped and reduced to mere numbers in a genocide that the rest of the world turned their face away from.

The blood of Bengali Muslims was also spilled, those who stood against the tyranny of West Pakistan and rejected Urdu for their mother tongue Bangla. And from their supreme sacrifice, Bangladesh was born. It was conceived as a country for both Hindus and Muslims and others with Bangla as the common language, Bengali culture as the glue between citizens of different faiths.

By 1985, more than US$ 12 million had been sent to Bangladesh, money raised from the album and the film after the concert. The Concert for Bangladesh opened the eyes of the world to the atrocities in East Pakistan. The world came to know of US President Nixon's support to West Pakistan that sent its army to crack down on East Pakistan's Bengalis, Hindus and Muslims both.

In 1972, the UN honoured Ravi Shankar, Harrison and Harrison's manager Allen Klein with the 'Child is the Father of Man' award for their efforts. The Concert for Bangladesh became a blueprint for star musical events for the cause of humanity in the years to come.[2]

'Mainly the concert was to attract attention to the situation ... The money we raised was secondary, and although we had some money problems ... they still got plenty ... even though it was a drop in the ocean. The main thing was, we spread the word and helped get the war ended,' George Harrison said later.[3]

But did the war of 1971 end?

Yes, East Pakistan got separated from West Pakistan, became an independent country and named itself Bangladesh. Yes, it adapted the first ten lines of Rabindranath Tagore's poem 'Ámar Sonar Bangla' as its national anthem:

My golden Bengal, thee I love.

Forever thy skies be, thine air like a flute set my heart in tune;

O Mother, aroma of mango orchard in Falgun driveth me crazy,

Ah, such miraculousness!

O Mother, time seeth in Ogrohayon smiles sweet all through fields of paddy—

But from the poison seeds that led to the bloodbath of 1971 do shoots of religious hatred still rise in Tagore's golden Bengal?

To mark the fifty-first anniversary of Mukti Judho, Bangladesh Liberation War, the India Today Group commissioned a series of special stories on the excesses of the West Pakistani regime that had launched Operation Searchlight—a state-sponsored pogrom to crush the war of independence. It had sparked a mass Hindu refugee movement to India.

Sahidul Hasan Khokon told us he fell sick revisiting 1971 through the oral histories and written accounts of survivors to write the special stories for *India Today*. Given below is a chapter from Sahidul's narrative in *India Today*[4]:

> They brought them [Hindus] to the school ground, lined them up, tied their hands and started raining bullets on them. They didn't stop at that. The barbarians poured kerosene on dying men and set them on fire. If anyone moved or made a sound, they shot him again and stabbed him with the bayonet.'
>
> It was May 26, 1971 when the Pakistan Army gunned down as many as 94 Hindus at the Burunga High School in the nondescript Burunga village in Burunga union of Balaganj upazilla of Sylhet district … This was in the third week of May 1971, as the war of Independence was at its peak.
>
> Terrified Burunga villagers met Burunga Union Chairman Injad Ali. On the afternoon of May 25, Injad

> Ali and Chief of the Union Peace Committee Soyef Uddin Master made an announcement in Burunga and neighbouring villages that a Peace Committee would be formed in Burunga High School the next day (May 26). They said Peace Committee identity cards would be distributed to villagers.
>
> Everyone was given the assurance that the Pakistani forces would not harass or torture those who had identity cards from the peace committee.

Carrying the identity card would mean that the villagers had nothing to do with the war. They would be able to move around freely. Little did the villagers know that the Peace Cards would not hold back barbarians at the gate.

Shahidul's narrative continues:

> [...] the villagers—both Hindus and Muslims—attended the committee meeting at Burunga High School on May 26 morning.[5]
>
> More than 1,000 people gathered at the school around 8 am. The peace committee started making a list of villagers present in the room. Around 9 am ... Pakistani forces arrived at the the school ground, accompanied by Abdul Ahad Chowdhury, the commander of Razakar of Karansi village,[6] and Abdul Khalek, a village doctor.
>
> The Pakistani army men took the list from members of the Peace Committee. A group of Pakistani forces checked every house in the village and forced the

> remaining men, who did not come to the Peace Committee meeting, to come to the ground in front of the school.
>
> [...] Thousands of people were present at the school, with fear writ large on their faces ... Razakars, Pakistan Army and members of the Peace Committee separated the Hindus and Muslims by checking the list.
>
> Hindus were taken to the office room of the school, while Muslims to a classroom. Both the Hindu and Muslim groups were taught the Kalima and asked to sing Pakistan's national anthem. Around 9.30 am ... ordered everyone to deposit all the money they had as well as gold jewellery, most of the Muslims were released.
>
> Pakistan Army men asked 10–12 Muslims to bring nylon rope from the local market ... The Hindus were asked to knot them together tightly. Some Hindus ... started screaming.
>
> Pritiranjan Chowdhury, a teacher of the school, who survived the massacre, said, '[...] I was supposed to go to the school around 8 am on May 26, I got a little late. When I reached there, I saw all the Hindus locked upc ... Seeing me, they caught me and took me to the office room. A window in the room was a little broken ... I somehow opened the window and managed to jump out of it.

Seeing this, some other Hindus also ran away after he did. Those who could not run away with Pritiranjan

Chowdhury or did not have their god watching over them, were shot down.

> Shri Nivas Chakraborty, another survivor who was shot twice in the Burunga massacre, said, "[…] As soon as a gunshot hit my left hand , I feigned that I was dead, and lay still on the ground. When the army men left after the firing, some wounded men stood up."[7]

They did not know they would come back to check! They were shot at, again. Another bullet grazed Shri Nivas Chakraborty's skin but he survived. His father and brother died.

> After unleashing violence, the Pakistani soldiers and the Razakars asked Sylhet court lawyer Ram Ranjan Bhattacharya to leave, As soon as the sick Ram Ranjan stood up from his chair, the marauders shot him dead.[8]

The houses in the village were then set on fire to bring to the ground whatever was left standing.

How different are stories of massacres? How do you distinguish one act of barbarity from another? The other story by Sahidul Hasan Khokon that stood out among the series he wrote for *India Today,* was on the killings of Marwari Hindus during 1971—killings that time and history writers have forgotten.

But Nijhu Kumar Agarwal remembers.

> Fifty years back, he, along with the men and women of this community were deceived by the Pakistan Army into believing that they would be sent back to their motherland through a train and spared the genocide unleashed on Bengalis.
>
> This group of Marwaris numbered … numbered around 450.[9]

They had no skin in the game. They were not fighting to retain Bangla as the language and Bengali culture as the raison d'etre in this part of the world. They were businessmen who did not trade on brutalized bodies.

> As announced on loudspeakers that they had to board the last train back home to India, they got on it past midnight from Saidpur in Nilphamari, where they had settled for business over the years.
>
> The train, believed to be heading for Jalpaiguri in West Bengal through the Chilahati border … and came to a halt near railway culvert No. 338 in the Golahat area, only two kilometers away from where they had started. All the compartments were shut from the outside. Peeping through a hole, they could see Muslim Biharis equipped with weapons and Pakistani Army men who would soon butcher them to death. All hell broke loose—[10]

Armed men jumped out, took away the women by force, as the men pleaded. Once the women were separated, the men were stabbed. Some pleaded that they be shot instead of being stabbed. They were told Pakistan's bullets were not so cheap to be wasted on them. The night turned red as bodies piled up on railway tracks. Eight to ten boys managed to escape with shrieks of elders ringing in their ears. Nijhu Kumar Agarwal was one of them. What he saw that day would stay with him forever.

'We talk about Bengalis. But those bastards didn't spare even these Marwaris,' Sahidul Hasan Khokon tells us in anger. 'I broke down talking to survivors, women and men who were broken that day never to be whole again but lived to tell the tale.'

Sahidul's narrative states: 'The genocide orchestrated and masterminded by Pakistan, began on the night of March 25, 1971 … Three million were killed, 200,000 to 300,000 women were violated in the most diabolic ethnic cleansing since the days of the Holocaust.'[11]

And these are just rough estimates. How much does the world or even the subcontinent talk about it?

The Unbearable Burden of Being a Hindu

Like Sahidul Hasan Khokon, Anthony Mascarenhas met survivors of the 1971 carnage. Unlike him, Mascarenhas also met those who did not survive! His exploits during the 1971 war, were brought to light in an article by Ashis Ray in the *National Herald*, in 2021.[12] In 1971 Mascarenhas was the Pakistan correspondent of *Sunday Times*, London, while also working as an Assistant Editor with the Karachi newspaper *Morning Times.* The Pakistan Army had given him the chance to see their East Pakistan operation, like embedded journalists from CNN and other media houses in America's war against terror in Iraq and Afghanistan.

When Mascarenhas questioned why the soldiers of the 9th Division (of G-2 Ops posted near Comilla in East Pakistan) on patrol were planning to shoot dead the slight young man they had spotted running away, their Major said it straight:[13]

> "Because he might be a Hindu or he might be a rebel, perhaps a student or an Awami Leaguer. They know we are sorting them out and they betray themselves by running."
>
> "But why are you killing them? And why pick on the Hindus?"
>
> "Must I remind you", [Major] Rathore said severely, "how they have tried to destroy Pakistan? Now under the cover of the fighting we have an excellent opportunity of finishing them off."
>
> "For God's sake don't shoot," I cried. "He's unarmed. He's only a villager."
>
> Rathore … fired a warning burst. As the man sank to a crouch … two jawans were already on their way to drag him in.
>
> […] The Major asked: "Who are you?"
>
> "Mercy, Sahib! My name is Abdul Bari. I am a tailor from the New Market area in Dhaka."

"Don't lie to me. You're a Hindu. Why were you running? Tell me the truth. Why were you running?"

The man couldn't answer. A jawan took his lungi off him. His circumcized penis saved his life. Indeed, he was not a Hindu. That poor tailor from Dhaka lived. Many didn't.

Being Hindu in East Pakistan in 1970 and 1971 meant death. Ashis Ray quotes Mascarenhas who wrote:

> For six days I travelled with the officers of the 9th Division headquartered at Comilla. I witnessed at close quarters the extent of the killing. I saw Hindus, hunted from village to village and door to door, shot off-hand after a cursory "short-arm inspection" showed they were uncircumcized.[14]

Mascarenhas wanted the world to know what was happening in East Pakistan. On the face of it, West Pakistan wanted East Pakistan to not become independent. But it was a war to wipe out the Hindu-ness of being. Even when you converted to Islam you had to prove you retained nothing Hindu.

'This is a war between the pure and the impure … The people here may have Muslim names and call themselves Muslim. But they are Hindu at heart … We are sorting them out … Those who are left will be real Muslims. We will even teach them Urdu.'[15]

The Pakistani Army launched Operation Searchlight for complete cleansing of the Bengali and Hindu identity. Even the press secretary of the third president of Pakistan, Yahya Khan, said that this operation was to 'brainwash the people, wean them off their Bengali mores and make them true Pakistanis … The Hindu influence must be eradicated root and branch and the people who were misguiding the innocent and illiterate masses must be liquidated.'[16]

Yahya Khan, who served as the President of Pakistan from 25 March 1969 to 20 December 1971 let Pakistani soldiers kill and rape as many as they could. One Pakistani soldier was proud he had killed 932 people himself. Armed Pakistani soldiers boasted they had demolished an entire Hindu neighbourhood in one night, and killed at least 10,000. Many journalists saw this with their own eyes, but few had courage like Mascarenhas to report what they saw.

Ashis Ray wrote that Mascarenhas reached the *Sunday Times* office in London on 18 May 1971, met Harold Evans, the editor, and told him he wanted to write a big story about what was going on in Pakistan and why nearly five million people had already fled to India from East Pakistan. He knew South Asian newspapers wouldn't report the story because of power dynamics. He wanted the *Sunday Times* to publish the truth. *Sunday Times* ran Mascarenhas' report with the headline 'Genocide' on 18 May 1971. Before the story came out, Mascarenhas escaped from Pakistan.[17]

A 'Gaddar' Remembers!

'Jinnah's Pakistan had, by then, turned into kabarstan. It was just twenty-four years since the birth of Pakistan, and it was in a shambles by the time Operation Searchlight was launched.'

This comes to us straight from the horse's mouth, retired Lieutenant Colonel Quazi Sazzad Ali Zahir. The Great Gaddar. Or, the Soldier with a Bleeding Heart. What you think he is, depends on who you are. India and Bangladesh think he is a hero. Quazi Sazzad Ali Zahir was given the Independence Award, Bangladesh's highest civilian award in 2013 and India's fourth highest civilian award, the Padma Shri, on 9 November 2021.

Pakistan would probably shoot him in the head!

We met Quazi Sazzad Ali Zahir inside a news channel office in Dhaka in September 2022. He had come for a talk show and had some time to spare for us before the show began.

Sazzad Ali Zahir joined the Pakistan Army in 1969. He was in his twenties then and still too young and humane to not be affected by Operation Searchlight, a part of which he became. He saw men being shot and women being raped. He saw Hindus being killed simply for being Hindu. This was not a war he signed up for. Sazzad Ali Zahir flipped. He decided to leave Pakistan and join East Pakistan's war of liberation. The 'Great Gaddar' recalled that he crossed the border in East Pakistan and entered India 'with Pak

Army deployment maps stuffed inside my boots and Rs 20 in pocket'.

Nobody wanted to believe his story. Everyone he met this side of the border thought he was a Pakistani spy. After many interrogations, Indian Army officials were finally convinced he wanted to fight for the liberation of East Pakistan and sent him back with help. Sazzad Ali Zahir actively participated, organizing the 2nd Artillery Force under Sector 4 in the Sylhet region.

The Indian government gave six 105 mm artillery guns to the Mukti Bahini and with that a field artillery battery was formed. It was named the Raushan Ara Battery. Sazzad Ali Zahir became the co-captain. From October 1971, the battery started assisting the Mukti Bahini Z Force in the greater Sylhet region with artillery fire support.

'Let me tell you there were many Bengali Muslims fighting for the Pakistani Army,' he told us. 'Many Bengali army officials became our enemies. The ones who had left Pakistan Army to fight for the birth of a new country were mostly Majors or below the rank of Major. The Mukti Bahini had one big problem. The Majors and other officers below them were young and enthusiastic, but lacked strategic knowledge of the battlefield. They had to be trained. And there was hardly anyone to train them. Only fifteen Bengali Muslim officials of higher ranks came to East Pakistan to fight for Bangladesh.'

Many of those Bengali Muslims who never wanted East Pakistan to win the war against West Pakistan are still in Bangladesh.

'Many traitors, who fought against Mukti Bahini in 1971, were allowed to come to Bangladesh and live here in peace. Their families requested Bangabandhu Mujibur Rahman to allow those Pakistani military personnel to return after the war. Bangabandhu was soft hearted. He allowed them to come back.'

Could Bangladesh become what Bangabandhu had wanted it to become, we asked.

'The traitors started crawling back to Bangladesh,' Sazzad Ali Zahir replied. 'Some of them even got membership of the Awami League. This eventually led to the assassination of Bangabandhu.'

The age of darkness that Bangladesh slipped into after the assassination of Bangabandhu saw many freedom fighters being dismissed. Sazzad Ali Zahir was one of them. Without a stable job, but with a family to feed, he suffered for the next twenty years. Things only got better after Sheikh Hasina, Mujib's daughter, became the Prime Minister of Bangladesh.

'One day I got a call from the Prime Minister's office. As soon as I got into the room, Sheikh Hasina said she knew of the unbearable trouble I had gone through. She wanted to do something for me and my family. I didn't say anything to her for few seconds. Then I said I don't need anything. I asked her to make Bangladesh the beautiful country that her father had envisioned. Yes, 1971 didn't end. East Pakistan had many internal enemies who wanted it to remain a part of West Pakistan. Bangladesh today still has snakes who want this country to stop being what it is. They are inimical to our culture, our language. Our secularism. They are inimical to Hindus.'

How Pakistan Saw Hindus

How does Pakistan remember 1971?

The Hamoodur Rahman Commission of Inquiry was appointed in the December of 1971 to find out:

> [...] the circumstances in which the Commander, Eastern command, surrendered and the members of the Armed Forces of Pakistan under his command laid down their arms and a cease-fire was ordered along the borders of West Pakistan and India and along the cease-fire line in the State of Jammu and Kashmir.[18]

The commission examined 213 witnesses and after six months, submitted a report in July 1972. The report was not shared with the public in Pakistan.

The evidence given by Lt. Col. Aziz Ahmed Khan (Witness no. 276), who was Commanding Officer (CO) of 8 Baluch and then CO of 86 Mujahid Battalion, show how Pakistan saw Hindus in East Pakistan:

> Brigadier Arbab … also told me to destroy all houses in Joydepur. To a great extent I executed this order … General Niazi visited my unit at Thakurgaon and Bogra. He asked us how many Hindus we had killed. In May, there was an order in writing to kill Hindus'

> This order was from Brigadier Abdullah Malik of 23 Brigade.[19]

The exodus during the Liberation War in 1971 was largely fuelled by a pattern of 'selective genocide'. So, it is important to assert the difference between the socio-cultural identities of 'Bengali' and 'Hindu Bengali'. There is a pattern of selective violence in the Pakistan Army's attacks on the night of 25 March 1971. This has gone down in the pages of history books as Operation Searchlight.

What was it they were searching for?

In Dhaka, for instance, Pakistan Army officials and Razakars attacked five or six places on the night of 25 March. Places like Rajarbag, Pilkhana and even Dhaka University campus were hotspots for Mukti Bahini fighters and free thinkers. Hence, the Pakistani attacked these places.

Why Jagannath Hall, a residence hall for minority students, mostly Hindus? Why Ramana Kali mandir in Dhaka, a place where Hindu devotees congregated? Why Shakhari Patti, the area where shells and bangles were made for Hindu women?

The answer is simple: Because these were Hindu areas. Archer Blood, then US' consul general in Dhaka, wrote:

> We were also harboring, all of us were harboring, Bengalis, mostly Hindu Bengalis, who were trying to flee mostly by taking refuge with our own servants. Our servants would give them refuge. All of us were doing

> this. I had a message from Washington saying that they had heard we were doing this and to knock it off. I told them we were doing it and would continue to do it. We couldn't turn these people away. They were not political refugees. They were just poor, very low-class people, mostly Hindus, who were very much afraid that they would be killed solely because they were Hindu.

As they got to know being Hindu meant death, many started taking new names.

Dhaka's Sushil Sutradhar gave a statement which is mentioned in '*Hindu Janagosthir Ekattar*':

> We got know the Pakistani Army is looking for Hindus. We decided to leave our houses and take shelter in the vacant staff quarter of Ajimpur on March 28. But we didn't stay there for long. Pakistani Army would march in anywhere and inquire about the identity of those staying inside. Next, we went to stay at 27, Dhanmondi Road in Dhaka. But we also decided to change our names. Sushil Sutradhar became Farukh Hussain. My sister-in-law became Saleha Begum.[20]

It is amazing how this 'selective genocide' didn't cause as much uproar in India and the rest of the world as it should have. It turned citizens into refugees who sought shelter in India. An official estimate shows nearly "90 per cent of refugees coming in 1971 to India from East Pakistan were Hindus."[21]

> Of the total population of East Pakistan only 16 or 17 per cent were Hindus, and a huge chunk came to India seeking refuge. The Indian government never brought this out in public domain but it was recorded that "by the middle of June, there were 53,30,000 Hindus, as against 4,43,000 Muslims and 1,50,000 refugees from other religious groups."[22]

The Hindus were simply afraid to go back. All India Congress Committee (AICC) sponsored a delegation led by Sucheta Kripalini and other members like Rama Reddy, Chaudhury A. Mohammed and B.L. Mohanty. In June 1971, they visited refugee camps that had come up across West Bengal in areas like Badhuria, Narainpur, Hasnabad, Moitra Bagan, Taki and Thuba. They saw for themselves the deplorable condition of the refugee camps, heard from the refugees the horror they had escaped from and tried to gauge their plans for the future. Then they released a statement for the press:

> The party spoke to the leader of one group Laxmikant Biswas of Goalpara village, Faridpur. He recounted similar story of cruelty, murder and abduction. He and his party were walking on foot for the last 7 days from Faridpur. On their query whether they could go back to East Bengal again, they said it was impossible.[23]

How could they possibly go back? Pakistani soldiers were killing Bengalis, especially Bengali Hindus. For the women, it was an unending nightmare. Joseph Fried, a correspondent for the *New York Daily News*, wrote what he saw and heard: 'Razakars swooped down on villages in the night, rounding up women by force. Some were raped on the spot. Others were carried to military compounds ... weeping survivors of villages told of how wives were raped before the eyes of their husbands—'

West Pakistan was trying to retain its pride but shaming East Pakistan.

As Scott Butcher, the junior political officer in the US consulate in Dhaka, would say later, 'They (Pakistan) know that India was the midwife of Bangladesh. They defeated the military, which is proud. That was a real sock in the gut for Pakistani dignity. They lost half their country and more than half their population.'[24]

When the war ended and Bangladesh became a free country, many of these Hindu refugees went back. What do they feel today?

We meet Bibhutibhusan Biswas at Bagula in the Ranaghat subdivision of Nadia district in West Bengal. He is a Bangladeshi citizen and had come to visit a relative in India. On a November afternoon in 2022, in a house in a village set amidst the green and grey of rustic Bengal, he offers us lunch. We ask for tea, and then Bibhutibhusan Biswas takes us back to 1971.

A student of class eight, Biswas had come to this side of the border with his family to escape the genocide. When the war was over, the family decided to go back. Biswas was too young to have an opinion then. Today, he says they made a mistake. 'We should have appealed to Indira Gandhi for citizenship in 1971. We shouldn't have gone back,' the retired primary school teacher from Bangladesh tells us.

'The Pakistani Army mainly targeted the malayans in 1971.[25] My father fell for the secular dream for Bangladesh. We were short-changed,' Biswas tells us.

So what really changed for Hindus in East Pakistan when Bangladesh was born?

'The idea of Bangladesh is a beautiful lie,' replies Mrityunjay Devvrat.

We have come to meet him at the Vasant Vihar Club in South Delhi, which is close to where he stays. Devvrat is not a household name, yet, among cinema watchers in India, his 2014 film *Children of War* based on the 1971 Bangladesh genocide and the Bangladesh Liberation War, had created quite a flutter in both India and Bangladesh.

The man in a ponytail, who drops one truth bomb after another, takes a long drag from his cigarette and resumes the tale of the tale he put up on the big screen. 'The lie [the idea of Bangladesh] was born in 1971 after eight months, two weeks and six days of the Bangladesh Liberation War, roughly the same time needed to give birth to a human baby. Here, a new nation was born amidst beautiful songs and fine principles, but the depravity that marked its birth also cast a very dark shadow over its future.'

His film received a positive review from the famous film critic Subhash K. Jha, who said: 'It is impossible to believe that this war epic has been directed by a first-time filmmaker. How can a virgin artiste conceive such a vivid portrait of the rape of a civilization?'

Critics were kind, but the Jamaat was not amused with Devvrat after his film was dubbed in Bangla and released across nearly sixteen cinema halls across Bangladesh in Dhaka, Rajshahi, Sylhet, Joydebpur and Tangail. 'There were protests in Bangladesh against the film and also in West Bengal. I got threats from Jamaat leaders hiding in West Bengal also. Guess I managed to rip off the band-aid and show the world the festering wound they gave!'

We ask him what made him think of such an unusual topic for his first film. He asks us instead why we are writing this book. We tell him what is now Bangladesh was once the land of our fathers and forefathers and that the mind cannot be partitioned even if countries can be. Devvrat smiles at the answer and says his parents were designers and their vocation took them to Bangladesh in search of handicrafts and travelling with them got him entangled in a fabric of a different kind—a social fabric that is forever in fear of being shred into pieces.

What did he find during his research for the film and his travels thereafter? What is the condition of the Hindu in Bangladesh?

Devvrat avoids the question but talks about how the research for the film made him sick, the fate of the 2,00,000 women raped, and the birth of thousands of war babies. The Pakistan Army and the Razakars also kept sex slaves inside Pakistan Army camps.

We try again. What did his research show? Were Hindu women subjected to worse treatment than Muslim women by the Pakistan Army?

'How do you say one type of rape was worse than the other type? Can you? When you look at 1971 you can! There were broadly four kinds of rape by the Pakistan Army on Bengali women. There were rapes to produce pure Pakistani children in that side of Pakistan. Then there were rapes by Pakistani officers for entertainment. There were rapes to spread terror. In this type of rape, the breasts of women were chopped off after the act. The Bengali Hindu women were mostly killed after rape because they would not have been able to give birth to pure Pakistani children due to their religion.'[26]

We sit in silence. Bengali Muslims and Hindus fought and suffered and died during 1971 for the idea of Bangladesh. Why is the Bengali Hindu in distress now that Bangladesh is a reality?

'Like I said, the idea of Bangladesh is a lie. A beautiful one, but a lie nonetheless,' Devvrat says.

Loving a Language to Death

Of the many prisms through which one can view the Bangladesh Liberation War of 1971, is as a 'selective genocide of minority Hindus'; and this prism has surprisingly been the most neglected one. Having said this, it cannot also be denied that the language movement in East Pakistan which began in 1952, as a rejection of Urdu for Bangla, was a cultural revolt with a fundamentally secular character.

The movement to make Bangla or Bengali the official language of East Pakistan was inevitable because the linguistic oppression of the Pakistan government (controlled from West Pakistan) prone to Urdu was vehemently rejected by the Bangla speaking majority of East Pakistan.

Given below is a table that shows the linguistic pattern of the Pakistani population in undivided Pakistan to contextualize the language movement, which began in 1952[27]:

Language	**East Pakistan (%)**	**West Pakistan (%)**
Urdu	1.3	14.6
Bengali	99.0	0.1
Punjabi	0.0	67.6
Sindhi	0.0	14.2
Pashto	0.0	8.9
Balochi	0.0	2.9
English	0.8	2.1

The language movement of East Pakistan drew impetus from the common Bengali language that was spoken by an overwhelming majority. However, the political elites in West Pakistan thought this movement was being powered by the minority Hindus, something unprecedented since the creation of Pakistan in 1947. West Pakistan felt Bengali Hindus would stand in the way of unifying East and West Pakistan with one unique language, Urdu. Liaquat Ali Khan, the first Prime Minister of independent Pakistan, had spoken in favour of Urdu in the Constituent Assembly of Pakistan on 25 February 1948.

Even Jinnah, Governor General of Pakistan in 1948, had addressed a large gathering in Dhaka, saying, 'Let me make it clear to you that the state language of Pakistan is going to be Urdu and no other language. Anyone who tries to mislead you is really an enemy of Pakistan.'[28]

In an Assembly debate Liaquat said Dhirendranath Datta—one of the few Congress leaders who chose to stay in Pakistan instead of India—should realize Pakistan was created because of the demand of a 100 million Muslims in the subcontinent. And what was the language of these hundred million Muslims? It was Urdu. So, Pakistan is a Muslim state and it must have Urdu as its lingua franca, the language of the Muslim nation.

People like Dhirendranath Datta were the cultural vanguards of the language movement in Eastern Bengal in 1950s. In the Assembly debate, where Liaquat spoke in favour of Urdu, Dhirendranath had said: 'Out of a population of 6 crore 90 lakh, 4 crore 40 lakh are Bengali speaking. What should the lingua franca be? It should be Bangla.'[29]

Dhirendranath Dutta was not alone. Bengali leaders like Sheikh Mujibur Rahman, Tajuddin, Kaji Kamal and other Bengali Muslims had also rejected Urdu for Bangla.

Love for Bangla turned Kaji Kamal from Alamdanga into a guerrilla leader who took up arms against the army sent by West Pakistan. He had never heard of Che Guevara. Or read the *Red Book* of Chairman Mao. He only knew Mao as the friend of Pakistan President Yahya Khan. Yet Kaji Kamal put together an army of his own, an army to fight for the Bengali language and to achieve political and economic sovereignty in East Pakistan.

Freedom of language was the backbone of the freedom movement of East Pakistan. 'Jay Bangla' became the catch phrase of millions of Bengalis, Hindus and Muslims both. *Assam Tribune*, an Indian English language daily newspaper published from Guwahati and Dibrugarh in Assam, wrote an interesting story on 20 December 1970. It said 'Jay Bangla' was so popular a phrase in East Pakistan even among students, that in schools they didn't greet teachers in classrooms by saying 'Present, Sir' anymore. They said: 'Jay Bangla'.

Fighting for freedom from imposed Urdu and a love for the Bengali language, led to the birth of Bangladesh in 1971. After 1971, Urdu schools were closed down. Urdu vanished from both primary and higher education. As an optional paper, Urdu had to be discontinued after 2002 as Urdu teachers and Urdu books were no longer available. But through the years, there has been a constant political pressure to regularize Urdu in Bangladesh, a country formed after rejecting Urdu!

It started with a constitutional amendment in 1975 that replaced the phrase 'Bengali Nationalism' with 'Bangladeshi

Nationalism'. It continues through the spurt in the number of Qwami madrasas that adopt their own syllabus with predominantly religious content that greatly emphasizes Arabic, Persian and Urdu language studies.

No language should be abolished from any land. The romance of a foreign tongue can never be overemphasized. What should not perhaps be underemphasized is the reason why East Pakistan became Bangladesh—rejecting Urdu for Bangla, embracing the syncretic Bengali identity over a religious identity. As demand for Urdu goes up, as attacks on Hindus continue to make headlines in modern-day secular Bangladesh, one wonders if 1971 has seeped through the intervening decades and come to haunt our present.

8

A FATHER'S DREAM, A DAUGHTER'S CHALLENGE

INSIDE A LIGHT blue rectangular room, stands a young man with thick, black-framed glasses, his back to the wall. From the lone window light falls on one side. What is the man thinking? He is thinking about his friends who tell him to write his story when they come to visit him. He is thinking about his fellow journeymen who want him to record the events that dot his political life for posterity. The year is 1967. The place is Dhaka Central Jail.

We turn the page. The young man is still inside the blue box. He is still thinking. Eyes closed, he thinks of the time his wife came to visit him in jail. Holding the bars that separate them she tells him to write his story, now that he has nothing else to do. The young man tells himself the wife does not know that he has not been able to achieve anything. He has only been able to make a small sacrifice for the sake of his beliefs and his ideals. What else has he been able to do that he should pen down?

Next page. The young man is still inside his blue room in Dhaka Central Jail. Night has fallen and the *jamadar* puts a lock on the door of his cell from outside and leaves for the night. The young man looks out of the tiny window of his room into the night sky. A face looms large into his mind, the face of Huseyn Shaheed Suhrawardy. The young man remembers how he got to meet Suhrawardy, come close to him, learn from him. Thoughts of Suhrawardy's finally compel the young man to write his story.

Another page. The little blue rectangle box is now a whole page. The young man is at the centre of the page, sitting on a cot, furiously putting his thoughts down on paper. A large quote bubble appears over his head to reflect his thoughts. From the quote bubble we read that the young man is thinking about his wife whose nickname is Renu. Renu had bought notebooks for him to write on and deposited them with jail authorities. After examining them, the authorities have handed the young man those notebooks. Renu had come again to plead with him to write his story. The young man finally decides to do so.

The young man is the hero of the graphic novel *Mujib*. We have paraphrased the first three pages of the first part of the ten-part graphic novel series *Mujib*. The series is published by the Centre for Research and Information (CRI), a not-for-profit policy research organization.

The hero of the graphic novel series, *Mujib*, is also the hero of Bangladesh, Sheikh Mujibur Rahman. Bangladesh *is* because of him and what Bangladesh will become may well depend on whether it embraces or rejects what his dreams were.

Mujib, the graphic novel series, has been edited by Shibu Kumar Sheel, a Bangladeshi Hindu, for whom Sheikh Mujibur Rahman's dream of a secular nation is the only hope to live for. An estimated 13.1 million Hindus in Bangladesh, out of its 165.16 million population, share Sheel's hopes.

Sheikh Mujibur Rahman had famously said:

> This country does not belong to Hindus. This country does not belong to Muslims. Whoever thinks this country is theirs, this country will be theirs. Whoever will feel happiness seeing this country prosper, this country will be theirs. Whoever will cry seeing this country sad, this country will be theirs. This country will also belong to those who have given away everything for this country's freedom and would do so in the future.[1]

These words are splashed on the inner walls of the Bangladesh Visa Office in Salt Lake, Kolkata, perhaps to tell Indians about to visit Bangladesh what the country stands for.

And it all started inside a jail cell.

Sometime early in 1966, Sheikh Mujibur Rahman penned the following lines to record his time in jail[2]:

> I was arrested soon after Pakistan was born. The year was 1948 and I was involved in the language movement. A year later, in 1949, I was arrested again, only to be let out in 1952. Hassled, my mother asked me: 'Babu, you have always spoken out in favour of this new country called Pakistan. You have spent all your money for the political movement that led to the birth of this country. Ordinary people of this country got to know why "Pakistan" is important from you. Then why do the Pakistani government arrest you?'

On 10 June 1966, he was arrested again from a political gathering of labourers of the jute industry at Narayanganj in East Pakistan. This was his third arrest in 1966.

Mujibur spent most of his time in the 1960s in jail, often in solitary cells where he had no one to talk to. He remembered his mother's question that he did not have any answer to. A decade had passed since his old mother asked him why the Pakistani government had arrested him. Mujib still did not know how to console her. He wrote:

> I didn't know what to say to my simpleton mother who stays in a village. I said, 'One day I will tell you everything.' That one day came and I told my mother everything about what we were doing. She could hardly

> understand. All she said was: 'One day you take me to the people who arrest you. I will shout at them.' My siblings laughed at her.[3]

Mujib's mother should have known these arrests were inevitable, given that Mujib was changing the very course of history. His political journey had begun decades ago, during the 1930s. As the head of a students' delegation, he had met Abul Kasem Fazlul Huq and Huseyn Shaheed Suhrawardy. Huq, popularly known as Sher-e-Bangla or Lion of Bengal, was a Pakistani Bengali lawyer and writer who presented the Lahore Resolution which had the objective of creating an independent Pakistan. (He also served as the first and longest Prime Minister of Bengal during the British Raj.) Suhrawardy was a Bengali barrister and politician who, as mentioned earlier, served as the Prime Minister of Pakistan from 1956 to 1957, and before that as the Prime Minister of Bengal from 1946 to 1947 in British India.

In Pakistan, Suhrawardy is revered as one of the country's founding statesmen. In Bangladesh, Suhrawardy is remembered as the mentor of Bangladesh's founding leader Sheikh Mujibur Rahman. In India, he is seen as a controversial figure; some hold him responsible for the 1946 Calcutta Killings. In India, he is also remembered for his performance as the Minister for Civil Supply during the Bengal famine of 1943.

Mujib would not turn his back on politics after the meeting. Suhrawardy became his mentor and the Muslim League his chosen path. Like millions of others, Mujib would dream to see the sun rise in a new country. A country called Pakistan.

Those days, Mujib was enthralled by Mohammad Ali Jinnah and is said to have cycled to Delhi to meet him. The veracity of the story cannot be fact-checked today but this much is certain that Mujib ardently admired the founding father of Pakistan, at least till the birth of the new country.

Pakistan was born, a new battle in which this young Bengali Muslim League politician would pave the path for his people, both Hindus and Muslims, to speak their own tongue, value their cultural identity over their religious one. Fate would take Sheikh Mujibur Rahman, who once stood with Jinnah and Suhrawardy, beyond the idea of Pakistan, the idea of a nation for Muslims, towards a nation for Bengalis, irrespective of which god they prayed to.

He would carve out a secular country that spoke Bangla. He would call that country Bangladesh.

But let us slow down. Let us go back to 1952, when across East Bengal the idea of a Bengali acculturation was taking shape.

On January 27, when Khwaja Nazimuddin, then Prime Minister of Pakistan, declared Urdu to be the only national language, protest from all corners flared up in East Pakistan, reaching a peak on 21 February 1952 when lakhs of students gathered at the campuses of Dhaka University and other educational institutions in Dhaka, to raise their voice against the imposition of Urdu as the national language.

It was a civil disobedience movement for language. The police became so violent that it started firing on the protesting students. Abdus Salam, Abul Barkat, Rafiq Uddin Ahmed, Abdul Jabbar and Shafiur Rahman died in that firing, martyrs to the fight for the mother tongue. Many got grievously injured. The government had to deploy the army to control the situation on the ground.

A secular Bengali identity was overshadowing the religious identities of the East Pakistani people. East Pakistan was morphing, becoming more than what West Pakistan wanted it to be, soul searching, shape-shifting into something else.

Then, in 1963, the Awami Muslim League became Awami League by dropping the word 'Muslim'. No prizes for guessing that Mujibur Rahman was surely one of the most influential minds behind this change. The movement for language during this period was so spontaneous and so powerful that an amendment was made in the Pakistani constitution in 1956. Bengali was declared to be one of the state languages of Pakistan.

But that would not be enough.

21 February 1952 would come to become a rather special day for the people from then on. It was possibly for the first time in history that protestors would sacrifice their lives for the love of a language. Later, in memory, UNESCO would declare this day to be the International Mother Language Day. And like that, Bengali language came to become both the language and the foundation of Mujib's politics. Rejecting Urdu, for Bangla, would take him to his El Dorado, the mythical gold kingdom, his 'Sonar Bangla', his Bangladesh.

The birth centenary of Bengali literature legend Rabindranath Tagore was celebrated in East Pakistan in 1961, just as it was on the other side of the border, in India's West Bengal. But the Pakistani government had their aversion towards this. For them, Bengali language was essentially Hindu in nature and Rabindranath Tagore was but a Hindu poet.

Mujibur Rahman had by now become the undisputed leader of a secular Bengali constituency in East Pakistan, a critical mass becoming more and more powerful. By 1963, he had started referring to East Pakistan, formerly East Bengal, as 'Sonar Bangla' (Golden Bengal). He must have drawn from Rabindranath Tagore's famous song '*Amar Sonar Bangla, Ami Tomay Valobasi*' (O My Golden Bengal, I love Thee). This was composed during the partition of Bengal in 1905 by the British rulers of this subcontinent.

During his time in jail in 1967, Mujibur Rahman would recite Tagore's lines. He had several court cases against him. At times he would feel dejected and sing: '*Bipode more rokkha koro e nohe more prarthona/ Bipode ami na jeno kori voy* (That you protect me from danger is not my prayer/ That I shouldn't be scared to face danger is my wish.)'

Tagore's poems were floating in the air of 'Sonar Bangla' and Mujibur Rahman was in the heart of the Bengali people in East Pakistan. Hence, an inevitable ban followed in 1967 on 'Tagore's music all over Pakistan as a measure towards protecting Pakistan's "Muslim" Bengalis from what it considered the contaminating influence on Hindu culture as represented by the poet (Rabindranath Tagore).'[4]

Manash Ghosh, the Calcutta journalist of *The Statesman* newspaper, was given the assignment to cover political unrest in East Pakistan from the mid-1960s. The battle between Urdu and Bengali had become so evident by then, that the other Bengal, West Bengal, could not ignore it any more.

Ghosh's local contact in East Pakistan told him Urdu was being imposed in places where people wanted Bangla to prevail. The journalist remembers his contact telling him: 'Look at this Urdu welcome sign, "Khoshamded" (Welcome) written in Bengali script that greets visitors entering East Pakistan at this no man's land. We wanted "Swagatam" (also meaning welcome) to be written but it was considered too much of a Hindu welcome sign and was rejected.'[5]

On 5 December 1969, Sheikh Mujibur Rahman made an announcement:

> The very word 'Bangla' was attempted to be abolished forever from this country and from the topographical map of this country. Only apart from the Bay of Bengal, nowhere else the existence of 'Bengal' could be found. On behalf of the people of this province, I hereby declare that this eastern side of Pakistan will henceforth be known as 'Bangladesh'.[6]

Thus, Mujibur Rahman declared the secular Bengali identity to be the sole agenda of his politics. No surprise then that he became 'Bangabandhu' (The friend of Bengal).

For Mujib, the wheel had turned and how. He had stood with Jinnah once. He had stood with Suhrawardy. He had seen with his mortal eyes the mayhem in Calcutta for the birth of a nation for Muslims. That nation had been birthed. But the two parts of that nation, the West and the East, would no longer fit. And Mujib must fight again, this time not for a nation of Muslims, but for a nation of Bengalis, both Muslims and Hindus. East Pakistan would have to separate from West Pakistan for the love of Bangla, for the need for secularism.

But the birth of a secular state demanded sacrifices, and the imprisonment of Mujibur Rahman and others like him were the least of those sacrifices. Since the birth of Pakistan in 1947, Mujibur Rahman was arrested often any way. During his imprisonment in 1967, Mujib met one Nur Alam, a student of Dhaka University. Nur was a good student but he had to write his MA first year examination from inside the jail cell.

Mujibur knew him well, he knew the power of Alam's political oratory and his love for his land. He was the only son and would talk about his parents. Nur represented the voice of the Bengali youth from East Pakistan. There were others like Nur willing to put their lives on the line. Still in his early twenties, Nur Alam believed in revolution but also wanted to get out of captivity. One day he asked Mujib, 'Boss, what would happen to me if they set you free and I have to live here?'

Mujib replied like a leader of the people. 'Are you mad? They are not going to let me out any time soon. You be rest assured they will let all of you out before they release me.' Mujib told Nur Alam what the great American philosopher Henry David Thoreau had once said, 'Under a government which imprisons any unjustly, the true place for a just man is also a prison … Cast your whole vote, not a strip of paper merely, but your whole influence.'

Mujib believed Thoreau's words and assured Nur that he was happy in jail. He said it was better to be in jail in a State where there was no justice. Every once in a while, his wife and his children would come to meet him but they almost never asked if Mujib would be free any time soon. Instead, by mid-1960s, Mujib's daughter Sheikh Hasina would start following her father's political footprints.

She did what her father told her to do from jail.

In 1969, Mujibur wrote a letter to his daughter. This was a personal letter, but for Bangabandhu nothing was more personal than the dream of Bangladesh. Mujib wrote[7]:

> Take my love and affection. I had received Wazed's letter;[8] replied to him as well, perhaps he has received it. I didn't even get to see you properly after getting out of jail. Take care of your health. How is Wazed? We are all doing well. Don't ruin your health by worrying for me. Maybe you have heard that Manik bhai has suddenly died in Pindi. You can understand my condition. Professor Hai has also passed away. We have lost two valuable sons of Bangladesh. Don't worry. Sweden is a beautiful country. You all will like it. Do send letters.

The Professor Hai mentioned in the letter was a close associate of Mujibur Rahman and knew about the top-secret activities of Awami League leaders. There were others who also knew. Many of them were Hindus. Chittaranjan Sutar, a Hindu from Barisal, was one such close political associate of Mujibur Rahman. For Mujib, it was important to have India by his side and Chittaranjan Sutar was sent on an important mission. Sutar came to Calcutta on the eve of the 1970 election. Possibly his job was to locate a safe hideout in Calcutta for Awami League leaders and also to maintain a sound political relationship with the Indian government.

Manas Ghosh writes:

> He [Chittaranjan] was Mujib's personal pointsman in India. He had settled down in a large house in Bhowanipore's middle-class neighbourhood at 43, Rajendra Road, Northern Park area. His house, Sunny Villa, had turned into a beehive of Awami League activists in Calcutta. Anyone coming from Dhaka or elsewhere in Bangladesh and trying to meet Indian leaders or officers had to have his clearance.[9]

Mujib sought India's help since the end of the 1950s. Archival research suggests he had written a letter to Jawaharlal Nehru (India's Prime Minister till May 1964) seeking help. Sashanka S. Banerjee (a retired Indian diplomat who was close to Mujibur Rahman in the 1960s) writes about this in his book *India, Mujibur Rahman, Bangladesh Liberation & Pakistan*:

> Mujibur Rahman was now in his elements. He said that the purpose of calling the meeting was to hand over to me a top-secret letter to be forwarded to the Prime Minister of India in a diplomatic bag … I told him that apart from me, more importantly, it would be seen by two other officers in the Indian Diplomatic Mission in Dhaka before it was forwarded to the Prime Minister. Mujib asked who the two officers would be in the High Commission in Dhaka. With some hesitation but only to earn their trust I gave Mujib and Manik Mia the names: Mr Sourja Kumar Choudhury, the Deputy High Commissioner of India who was the Head of Mission in Dhaka and Colonel SC Ghosh, the Station Chief of Indian Intelligence in East Pakistan—[10]

Mujib wanted to end the West Pakistani dictatorship in East Pakistan in a democratic way. For this, voters of East Pakistan needed to cast their vote in favour of the Awami League in the 1970 election. The Bengali people, Hindus and Muslims, did just what their leader wanted.

Election day dawned on 7 December 1970 in Pakistan; the day the people of East Pakistan would speak up for Bangladesh through the ballot. It was the first of its kind election after the creation of Pakistan.

Political parties like the Awami League, Zulfikar Ali Bhutto's Pakistan People's Party, and three splinter groups of the Muslim League—the Jamaat-e-Islami (aka, Jamaat), the Jamiat-e-Ulema-e-Pakistan and the Jamiat-e-Ulema-e-Islam—contested in the election.

Bhutto was confident of victory.

Barely a month earlier, Bhola, the deadliest tropical cyclone ever recorded in human history and one of the world's deadliest natural disasters, had struck East Pakistan and India's West Bengal. At least 3,00,000 people died in the storm, possibly as many as 5,00,000, primarily as a result of the storm surge that flooded much of the low-lying islands of the Ganges Delta.

Who could have imagined another cyclone was waiting to hit the West Pakistani hukumat? Almost as deadly as Bhola, this political whirlwind changed political equations in Pakistan forever. The Awami League bagged 167 seats out of a total 313 in the Pakistan Assembly. In the Provincial Assembly, Mujib's party got a whopping 288 seats out of 300. What this meant was the birth of 'Bangladesh' was inevitable.

Election day had begun well for Bhutto. When the counting of votes started, it appeared that Bhutto would seize the day. But after midnight there was an unexpected Mujib wave and Radio Pakistan soon announced Mujibur Rahman was all set to become Pakistan's first democratically elected Prime Minister.

A story goes that after the election results were declared, Yahya Khan rang Bhutto to congratulate him for the Pakistan People's Party's performance in West Pakistan. A furious Bhutto shouted at him and said those bastard people of East Pakistan would now believe they deserved to rule the country!

If history was written by ballot boxes, yes, East Pakistan truly deserved to rule the country. But in the political history of South Asia, the bullet has often trounced the ballot. Yahya Khan went to Dhaka to reach an amicable settlement with Mujibur Rahman, it was too late in the day to dissuade secular Bengalis from a direct battle over what was rightfully theirs. West Pakistan could not digest the defeat. Bhutto and Yahya Khan were ready to stop Mujibur Rahman by any means.

Meanwhile, Bangabandhu had already given a clarion call to 7 crore Bengalis and on 7 March 1971 millions assembled at the Dhaka Race Course Maidan (today known as Suhrawardy Udyan). The crowd wanted to know their nation's future.

To avoid any possible attack on Mujib, who was facing death threats, two decoys wearing similar moustaches and Punjabi suits, got into two similar cars. Mujib was in the first car. His driver wanted to know what message he would deliver to the millions waiting for him. Mujib didn't really know what he would say to these people who had cast their vote so decisively for a secular Bengali nation. He is said to have replied, 'I don't know. I will just say what my mind tells me to say.'

That historical speech began with the line: 'My dear brothers and sisters, I have come here today with a heavy heart.' The remainder was about a possible battle for freedom. On the ground were posters with the words '*Ma-*

bonera astra dhoro, Bangladesh sadhin koro (O mothers and sisters, Pick your weapons to free Bangladesh)'.

Bangladesh was yet to be born. But Mujibur Rahman had begun controlling East Pakistan from 32 Dhanmondi, Dhaka, his residential quarters. He was giving directions to schools, colleges, administrative offices, industrial houses and even the banks in East Pakistan. Till 24 March 1971, there were several rounds of discussions and negotiations between Mujibur Rahman, Yahya Khan and Bhutto, but the West Pakistani leaders did not accept Mujib's six-point agenda.

Thus began a parallel government in East Pakistan, with the heart firmly placed inside 32 Dhanmondi. Twenty minutes after midnight on 26 March 1971 Bangabandhu, from his residence, announced the independence of Bangladesh saying[11]:

This may be my last message. From today, Bangladesh is independent. I call upon the people of Bangladesh wherever you might be and with whatever you have to resist the army of occupation to the last. Your fight must go on until the last soldier of Pakistan occupation army is expelled from the soil of Bangladesh and final victory is achieved.

Sheikh Mujibur Rahman had already hoisted the flag of an independent Bangladesh at his residence, on 23 March 1971. His announcement of Bangladesh's independence in the early hours of 26 March led to his arrest later that day. In March 1972, Jenefer Coates wrote, 'One of the first laws issued at dawn on 26th March through amplifiers in the streets of Dacca (Dhaka) decreed that anyone shouting Joi Bangla would be shot on the spot.'[12]

Fifty-one years later, on 11 September 2022 we stand before 32, Dhanmondi, Road 12, Dhaka, Bangladesh. Bangladesh's heart is still trapped inside this building, so easy on the eye for its structural simplicity, so heavy with the burden of history.

Night has fallen. It is too late for us to get in.

We walk the street that leads to the memorial.

On a slab of black stone are these lines: '*Jotokal Robe* Padma Meghna/ Gouri, Jamuna *Bahaman/ Totokal Robe Kirti Tomar/* Sheikh Mujibur Rahman. (As long as the rivers Padma, Meghna, Gouri, Jamuna flow, the tales of your deeds will be carried forward).'

We stand before the house where Mujib was killed on 15 August 1975. Mujib's killers also gunned down Sheikh Fazilatunnesa Mujib, his wife, who was killed upstairs; Sheikh Nasser, his younger brother, who was killed inside a lavatory; several servants, who were also killed in lavatories; Sheikh Jamal, his second son and an army officer; ten-year-old Sheikh Russel, his youngest son; and his two daughters-in-law.

In Dhanmondi, two other groups killed Sheikh Fazlul Haque Mani, Mujib's nephew and a leader of the Awami League along with his pregnant wife, Arzu Moni, and Abdur Rab Serniabat, Mujib's brother-in-law. They also killed a minister of the government and thirteen of his family members on Mintu Road.

On 12 September we enter 32, Dhanmondi. The house is now the Bangabandhu Memorial Museum. We meet Md. Nazrul Islam Khan, the curator, who deputes a staff member to take us on a tour of Bangladesh's most famous address.

As we go up the stairs, past walls that still have traces of the blood that was spilled, we ask ourselves the questions: What is the price of secularism, the price of imagining a country where Hindus and Muslims can stay as brothers? What is the price of rejecting Urdu for Bangla?

In their interview with Anthony Mascarenhas a year after Bangabandhu's murder, two of his killers, Lt Col Farooq Rahman and Lt Col Abdur Rashid, accepted they had killed Mujibur Rahman.[13] They seemed unapologetic, even proud of what they had done.[14] For them Bangladesh was 'not a viable state' and Mujibur Rahman had to take the blame for imagining it. They said they approached General Muhammad Zia-ul-Haq to get his help, but Zia didn't want to get involved directly.

Farooq Rahman said to the interviewer:

> Then we go up to the lawn and I told him that we are professional soldiers, we serve the country, we do not serve any individual. The army, the civil (service), the Government, everybody is going down the drain. We have to change it, we the junior officers, have already worked it out. We want your support and your leadership; and he said, I am sorry, would not like to

> get involved in anything like that. If you want to do something, the junior officers should do it themselves.[15]

From where they looked, Bangabandhu's murder was essential. It was essential to defeat what he stood for. Bangabandhu had not only envisioned but had given birth to a country solely on the principles of secularism linguistic identity. His murder was essential because he even acknowledged the sacrifices made by the Bengali women during 1970-71 and called them '*Birangona*' (heroines of the warfield).

Wkipedia states:

> During the 1971 Bangladesh Liberation War, members of the Pakistani military and Razakars raped between 200,000 and 400,000 Bengali women and girls in a systematic campaign of genocidal rape. Most of the rape victims of the Pakistani Army and its allies were Hindu women. Some of these women died in captivity or committed suicide while others moved to India. Imams and Muslim religious leaders declared the women "war booty". The activists and leaders of Islamic parties are also accused to be involved in the rapes and abduction of women.[16]

The Bangladesh government, under the premiership of Sheikh Mujibur Rahman, had formed a body to ensure the rehabilitation of these women. According to reports published in the *New York Times* on 12 May 1972, at least 1,500 women had applied for job training under the Rehabilitation Programme of the Bangladesh government.

Bangabandhu was also taking steps to start the process of toning down religious fundamentalism in Bangladesh. This made the fundamentalists so furious that they wanted to kill Mujib 'with 28 tanks, eighteen 105 mm guns and 700 men', which they did.

Syed Badrul Ahsan, who writes on politics and diplomacy, wrote:

> It was our moment of collective shame. All these decades after the cataclysm, we weep for Bangabandhu, for those who died with him. All those years ago, all of us willingly and willfully embraced cowardice and stayed home. A handful of uniformed murderers had commandeered the country. We let them.
>
> We live in the shadow of our shame. It is our sin. We will live in infamy because of the courage we did not show forty-seven years ago. It was our ingratitude toward our Leader that cast a sinister shadow across the land. We keep paying the price, close to five decades on. Our penitence at our sin goes on.
>
> Meanwhile, Dhanmondi 32 remains, as it will always remain, our claim to the glory that was Bangabandhu's politics, on the history that Bengalis forged for themselves in the defining era of the 1960s stretching into the 1970s.[17]

The inner walls of the building at 32 Dhanmondi Road bear testimony to the death of Bangabandhu's dream. It is too much to bear. We go to the rooftop and look out at free Bangladesh, Bangabandhu's dream land. Beneath this building is buried the nation's creator and his slain family. The baton of secularism is now in the hands of his daughter who escaped that day, Sheikh Hasina.

Sheikh Hasina and Sheikh Rehana were the only survivors of the brutal assassination of Sheikh Mujibur Rahman's family on 15 August 1975. They were in West Germany. In an interview with Smita Prakash, Indian news agency ANI's Editor-in-Chief, Sheikh Hasina recalled the last time she had met her family. 'Before leaving for Germany, I saw my father, mother, my three brothers, two newly-wedded sisters-in-law, everybody was in that house. They came to the airport to see us off. That was the last day, you know—'[18]

The two sisters shifted from Germany to New Delhi and lived in India for some time, but they had to hide their identity. There was a clear and present danger. Hasina also recalled her time in India:

> When we returned to Delhi, it was perhaps 24th August and I met Prime Minister Mrs Gandhi. She called us ... there we came to know that nobody is alive. She made all the arrangements for us, a job for my husband and the Pandara Road house. The first 2-3 years were so difficult to accept. My son was only

> four-years-old. My daughter, she's younger, both of them used to cry.[19]

Yes, Bangabandhu was killed but he had already planted his dream into the hearts of Bangladeshis. Sheikh Hasina went to the UK from where she started a movement against the autocratic rule in Bangladesh in 1980. It has been a long journey to reclaim Bangladesh's soul again, from the dictators and the fundamentalists. To put balm on the battered soul of the country's minority Hindu population that has gone down from 13.5 per cent in 1974 to 7.9 per cent in 2022.

On 7 January 2019, Sheikh Hasina entered the office of the Prime Minister for the fourth time. As we write the last pages of the book and Bangladesh gears up for its next General Election, Hasina stands out as the longest serving female leader in the world. But she has worn a crown of thorns all these years.

Sheikh Hasina was imprisoned in 1989, then in 1990 and later in 2007. The fundamentalists have made many attempts to kill her like they killed her father. There was a plan to kill her in police firing on 10 November 1987 during a 'gherao' programme of the Secretariat. Destiny saved Hasina, but many young Awami leaders were not so lucky. Nur Hossain, Babul and Fattah lay dead, as mayhem spread through Dhaka. The same day Sheikh Hasina's car was sought to be lifted by a crane, in front of the National Press Club.

On 24 January 1988 another attempt was made on her life when the police opened fire on her and charged the crowd with batons in front of the Chittagong Court Building. President Ershad was in power and many leaders and workers of the Awami League were killed. Hasina has also faced gunfire during her speeches at Laldighi Maidan, with her car once being shot upon while she was returning from a public meeting held there.

It got worse during the BNP's regime, with many attempts on her life. In one such attempt, on 11 September 1991, she was fired upon at a polling centre in the capital's Kalabagan area. In 1994 a series of gunshots hit her carriage at Ishwardi railway station while she was travelling by train. In 2000 two bombs, weighing 76 kg and 84 kg, were planted—one at the Kotalipara helipad and the other at her venue for a public meeting. She survived. The bombs were detected before she arrived.

The gravest attempt on her life so far, was the attack on 21 August 2004 when a dozen Arges grenades were thrown at her rally at Bangabandhu Avenue. She narrowly escaped but the attack left twenty-two leaders and workers of the Awami League dead, including central leader Ivy Rahman. Sheikh Hasina's hearing capability was impaired.

But what can possibly deter destiny's child? Hasina had heard of her family being wiped out and yet she decided to come back to Bangladesh. She had a job to do, she to carry forward the legacy of her father Bangabandhu.

Her father had drawn international attention with his speech at the United Nations General Assembly in 1974, and Hasina won UNESCO recognition for International Mother Language Day. Since the beginning of her second tenure as the Prime Minister of Bangladesh, Hasina has tried to rebuild Bangladesh keeping her father's vision at the forefront.

Journalist Subir Bhaumik wrote in 2021:

> Just before Hasina assumed power for a second time in 2009, the world had begun to talk of Bangladesh as 'another Afghanistan'. Not only were some Islamist radicals raising slogans as 'Bangla *hobe* Taliban' (Bangladesh will be Taliban), but the systematic Pakistani-style sponsorship of terrorism by Khaleda Zia's BNP and Jamaat-e-Islami government was threatening to take Bangladesh down the Pakistani Path.[20]

Keeping faith in secularism, remaining friends with India and having zero tolerance to terror, is what unites father and daughter. When the Prime Minister of Bangladesh touched the feet of one of the pioneers of the Language movement in a cultural programme on 21 February 2023, it came full circle.[21]

When a road in Dhaka was named after Indira Gandhi, when the Bangladesh government decided to honour the contribution of Indian soldiers by giving them the '*Muktijuddho Padak*' (Medal of Liberation), when the Indian Prime Minister Narendra Modi was made the special guest at the Golden Jubilee celebration of the Independence of Bangladesh, the circle came to a close.

But Mukta Das (see chapter 1) still has a question for Prime Minister Sheikh Hasina. Hate got her brother Jatan Saha killed during the 2021 Durga Puja violence in Noakhali. Political speeches on secular values won't bring her brother back. But her son, too young to know what separates Hindus from Muslims, saw his uncle being clobbered to death with his own eyes. That boy is today too afraid to get out of the house. 'Those men will come again for us,' he cries as he hides his face in his mother's lap.

Can the Bangladesh Prime Minister, the proud daughter of Bangabandhu Sheikh Mujibur Rahman, tell him they won't come back? Can she realize the dream her father dreamt? 'This country does not belong to Hindus. This country does not belong to Muslims. Whoever thinks this country is theirs, this country will be theirs—'

The Hindus in Bangladesh, 1.30 crore of them, are waiting for her answer.

NOTES

The detailed notes pertaining to this book are available on the HarperCollins *Publishers* India website. Scan this QR code to access the same.

INDEX

ABOUT THE AUTHORS

Deep Halder is a journalist and author. He has headed newsrooms across Delhi, Mumbai, Bhopal and Ahmedabad, and held top editorial positions in leading media outlets, including most recently as executive editor with *India Today*. Currently, he is working as contributing editor with The Print. He is the author of the bestselling book *Blood Island: An Oral History of the Marichjhapi Massacre* and *Bengal 2021: An Election Diary*.

Avishek Biswas is an assistant professor in English literature at Vidyasagar College under Calcutta University. He was awarded his doctoral degree from Jadavpur University for his thesis on the unheard voices of Namasudra Partition Survivors. His research interests include the history of Dalits in Bengal, Partition and Namasudra identity, Hindu migrants from Bangladesh, and the Liberation War in 1971.

HarperCollins *Publishers* India

At HarperCollins India, we believe in telling the best stories and finding the widest readership for our books in every format possible. We started publishing in 1992; a great deal has changed since then, but what has remained constant is the passion with which our authors write their books, the love with which readers receive them, and the sheer joy and excitement that we as publishers feel in being a part of the publishing process.

Over the years, we've had the pleasure of publishing some of the finest writing from the subcontinent and around the world, including several award-winning titles and some of the biggest bestsellers in India's publishing history. But nothing has meant more to us than the fact that millions of people have read the books we published, and that somewhere, a book of ours might have made a difference.

As we look to the future, we go back to that one word—a word which has been a driving force for us all these years.

Read.

Harper Collins

4th

HARPER PERENNIAL

HARPER BUSINESS

HARPER BLACK

हार्पर हिन्दी

HarperCollins *Children'sBooks*

HARPER DESIGN

HARPER VANTAGE

Harper Sport